Building a Birchbark Canoe

Building a Birchbark Canoe

The Algonquin Wâbanäki Tcîmân

David Gidmark
with a contribution by Denis Alsford

STACKPOLE
BOOKS

Published by
STACKPOLE BOOKS
5067 Ritter Road
Mechanicsburg, PA 17055

Printed in the United States of America

10 9 8 7 6 5 4 3 2 1

Cover photo by David Gidmark

Cover design by Mark Olszewski

Library of Congress Cataloging-in-Publication Data

Gidmark, David
    Building a birchbark canoe: the Algonquin wâbanäki tcîmân/David Gidmark with a contribution by Denis Alsford.
        p. cm.
    Includes bibliographical references and index.
    ISBN 0-8117-2504-9
    1. Abnaki Indians—Boats. 2. Abnaki Indians—Commerce. 3. Canoes and canoeing. 4. Boatbuilding. I. Alsford, Denis. II. Title.
E99.A13G53 1994
623.8'29—dc20
                                                                                        94-29643
                                                                                        CIP

To the memory of Edwin Tappan Adney

Contents

Acknowledgments

*T*his book might, in some ways, be considered an addition to the "Algonkin" and "Têtes de Boule" chapters of Edwin Tappan Adney's *The Bark Canoes and Skin Boats of North America*. Most material on the North American birchbark canoe is derivative of that pioneering work, published by the Smithsonian in 1964, fourteen years after Adney's death. My gratitude is herewith tendered.

Denis Alsford and I both owe thanks to the Canadian Ethnology Service, National Museums of Canada. In 1981, I received a grant under their Urgent Ethnology Programme to record the birchbark canoe building technique of Jocko Carle, River Désert Algonquin; Denis was the Curator of Collections for the National Museum of Man when he recorded the material that appears in Chapter VI. Denis and I sincerely thank the National Museums of Canada for allowing us to use the photographs of Daniel Sarazin in this book.

My debt to Denis Alsford is clear: Because of his fine skill and because there are almost no Indian birchbark canoe builders left, his record of Daniel Sarazin will probably remain the finest single documentation we have of these consummate native craftsmen.

Finally, Denis and I may have left something unspoken in the following pages that we should make clear here: We will be forever grateful for the privilege and the pleasure of having been able to work with Jocko Carle, William and Mary Commanda, James Jerome, and Daniel Sarazin.

I

The Evolution of the Algonquin Wâbanäki Tcîmân

*T*he origins of the birchbark canoe may forever be shrouded by the veil of time. Some historians believe that there is a link between the birchbark canoes of western Canada and those of Siberia, while others think that the craft may have been created independently in different regions.

There are several similarities between the birchbark canoes of western Canada and those of Siberia, particularly of the Amur River area in eastern Siberia. Otis Mason and Meriden Hill discuss these similarities in their book *Pointed Bark Canoes of the Kutenai and Amur*. An Amur River canoe in the collection of the Museum of Anthropology and Ethnography in St. Petersburg, Russia, exhibits two characteristics of western Canadian aboriginal canoes: It has widely spaced (20 to 25 cm, or 8 to 10 in.), fairly roughly finished ribs and wide (2 to 3 cm, or $^3/_4$ to $1^1/_4$ in.) spaces between pieces

Amur River birchbark canoe in the collection of the Museum of Anthropology and Ethnography in St. Petersburg. This canoe, which is made of a single sheet of bark, has nailed inwales and outwales, narrow, widely spaced ribs, and sheathing that does not completely cover the inner hull. On this canoe, the gores are not cut— the bark is crimped instead. (Photo by David Gidmark.)

of sheathing. Enough evidence exists to warrant a study of the possible very close connection between canoes of the two areas.

The birchbark canoes from the woodland regions of eastern North America, on the other hand, are characterized by a more intricate structure, fine woodwork, and a precise counterbalance of pressures. In eastern woodlands canoes, sheathing was either overlapping or edge-to-edge, unlike that of the Siberian canoe described above. Ribs were well finished and more closely (1 to 3 cm, or $^3/_8$ to $1^1/_4$ in.) and evenly spaced.

Might the birchbark canoe have come from Siberia with the ancestors of the North American Indians and then, in a fairly rudimentary form, spread to eastern North America from the west? Did it then undergo some influence, possibly foreign, that caused it to be refined into the striking craft still seen today in the territory of the Algonquin, Malecite, Abnaki, Ojibway, and others? Could the foreign influence possibly have been the Vikings? Strangely, the rib and planking structure of the eastern North American birchbark canoes is more similar to that of Viking ships than to those of Kootenay and Amur River canoes.

No solid evidence for this connection exists, but we do know that the Vikings were at L'Anse aux Meadows, Newfoundland, a millennium ago and that they likely ranged along the North American coast. Might they have influenced the master birchbark canoe builders of the region?

Adney seems to have believed that the birchbark canoe originated independently in separate regions of North America. He had intended in his excellent book *The Bark Canoes and Skin Boats of North America* to discuss migrations of prehistoric peoples in North America, as shown by the canoe. Regrettably, these theories were left out of this work posthumously by his editor.

Adney looked for the origins of the canoe not in birch bark but in elm, spruce, and similar forms of bark found in and beyond the birch areas. These could not be cut and sewn like birch bark, and the sheet had to be dealt with whole. The spruce bark and elm bark canoes were often heavy, and they were awkward and not durable. They had a rough framing of branches that frequently were unfinished. A long piece of wood was used for each

gunwale, and widely spaced branches formed rudimentary ribs. (At some point, the Iroquois, who had been using elm bark canoes, abandoned them in favor of the far more efficient birchbark canoe of the Algonquin. They ordered canoes from the Algonquin, and their preferred Algonquin canoe model was known as the *natowe tcîmân*.)

Adney classed canoes according to the way the builder achieved a bottom that was level and also wide enough for travel in shallow streams. This was done one way in the eastern woodlands; another way in the Athabascan area; and yet another in the west, where the canoes had pointed ends. Adney included in the western canoe classifications not only the Kootenays of British Columbia but also the Amur River canoes of Siberia.

Adney believed that the approximate stages of development of the bark canoe in the eastern woodlands were as follows:

1. The elm bark and spruce bark canoes with ties slight and at long intervals.

2. Primitive birchbark canoes, similar in body form to the elm bark and spruce bark canoes, but with gunwale attachments slight, allowing only a little compression.

3. Birchbark canoes with gunwale attachments strengthened for increased compression by ribs.

4. Birchbark canoes with the root wrappings close together, making the attachment stronger. But if the point of continuous wrapping was reached, as in the uninterrupted root lashing of a birchbark basket, it became evident that the rib, no matter how great the tension, was not secure in place with two gunwales.

Development then seemed to diverge in two different parts of the eastern woodlands. One area adopted the group system of close wrappings, with open spaces between where the rib ends found secure footing, while the other went to a single, rounded gunwale. This latter improvement created a recess for the rib ends, but the canoe was not as strong or durable as the former.

This caused Adney to form some theories:

If the elm-spruce type with its attachments at intervals is the prototype of all the eastern woodland canoes, the question arises: Did the central region group system of wrapping proceed directly from the elm-spruce canoe; or did the birchbark, as it evolved from the simpler type, assume the close-wrapped gunwale form first, which in the inner area changed to the present group system?

By elimination, the present group system was not borrowed from the northwestern people, whom we state were at the time Eskimo of the old Hudson Bay Eskimo culture. The collective evidence is rather that these original Eskimo people borrowed ideas from the St. Lawrence rather than the other way. For instance, sheathing as well as end form and construction of their large canoes. The borrowing was done at Lake Superior, and the contact covered such a period of time that we can more rightly say that Eskimo at Lake Superior and the St. Lawrence shared and contributed as well as received ideas developed in that area of intercourse, friendly or unfriendly, with whatever people, Algonkins or not, who occupied the southern region. Then they went away, and development went on. About the upper lakes, ideas developed further than the large Mackenzie canoes show.

It does not help the solution to suggest that group wrappings were borrowed from the Mackenzie canoes. That would oblige us to explain how the Mackenzie basin people changed from their own type of continuous wrapping.

The improvement effected by the group wrapping system was in strength and durability in so marked a way an improvement over the system of close wrapping, whether over two gunwales or one, that given conditions which called for such improvement, we can safely consider it developed from the close-wrapped canoe.

The next step in the long evolutionary process may have been the use of birch bark with the crude rib and gunwale structure. At some point, this gunwale assembly had to have been strengthened to support compression from the ribs. The refinements that followed over a long period of time eventually would have permitted the powerful rib compression characteristic of the modern craft. The finely finished ribs, sheathing, and gunwales of an Algonquin *wábanäki tcímán*, along with the ingenious structural balance of the components, may have evolved from the more rudimentary canoes.

Once birchbark canoes came into regular use, they were sometimes built for speed, for carrying capacity, or for stability in lakes, rivers, or along the seacoast. The smallest canoes were about 2.5 m (8 ft.) long. The Algonquin canoes ranged from 3.5 to 5.5 m (12 to 18 ft.) long. There was invariably an extremely shallow draught in relation to the length.

Some historians have advanced theories about how long the birchbark canoe has actually been in existence.

In *Indian Life in the Upper Great Lakes*, George Quimby writes of Indians of the Old Copper Culture (7000 to 3000 B.C.) that "birch bark was used for the manufacture of containers and probably many other things, including possibly canoes. . . . Indians of the Upper Great Lakes almost certainly had boats of some kind as early as 7000 B.C. We know this because some occupation sites have been found in areas that at the time would have been islands only suitable for summer living. . . . Probably these craft were wooden dugouts, but it is possible that the birchbark canoe existed by this time."

Though this use of the birchbark canoe is a possibility, transportation to these islands would have been possible not only using dugouts, as Quimby points out, but also using logs, rafts, or canoes of elm or spruce bark. It is interesting to note that the dugout canoe had a long life in terms of manufacture. Nineteenth-century lumbermen along the Ottawa River sometimes made dugouts of pine. In a number of cases, the lines appear to have been modeled after the *wábanäki tcímán*, the Algonquin canoe based on boats built by their neighbors to the east, the Abnaki.

There are not many traces of the birchbark canoe in the archaeological record. Excavations along the Ottawa River have revealed pre-Algonquin tools that may have been used in birchbark canoe making. On Morrison's Island, archaeologists discovered copper awls used five thousand years ago. Awls are essential to the construction of the birchbark canoe, but they had many other uses, and their discovery does not necessarily indicate canoe manufacture. Also found were beaver teeth ground at the ends to form left- and right-handed knives, possibly the antecedent to the steel-bladed crooked knife used in building birchbark canoes. These were also from five millennia ago. In addition, the site yielded stone gouges and adzes, indispensable to the manufacture of dugout canoes. The dugout canoe was undoubtedly made five thousand years ago and probably predated the birchbark canoe. On Allumette Island, not far from Morrison's Island, an archaeologist found "semi-lunar knives of slate," strongly suggestive of Indian crooked knives.

Though the origins of the birchbark canoe may remain forever impossible to determine, the very important part played by the Algonquin in the use and manufacture of the form of embarkation that opened up the continent is documented in history, especially since the arrival of the Europeans.

Champlain was responsible more than anyone else for the adoption of the birchbark canoe by the Europeans. In 1603 he encountered Indians (including Algonquin) near present-day Québec. He was particularly impressed by the speed of the birchbark canoes and felt that they would become essential to exploration and commerce. Indeed, for centuries the birchbark canoe remained the most important vehicle for the exploration of Canada. Anders Chydenius, a Finnish writer of the 1750s, observed that the French of Canada would not trade their canoes even for barrels of gold.

The first Indian canoe makers with whom the French had long-term contact were the Algonquin. Because of this, as well as its bow profile, the Algonquin canoe is thought to have been the model after which the fur trade canoes were built. The French lengthened the Algonquin birchbark canoe to produce the fur trade canoe, which often measured nearly 11 m (36 ft.) in length. These longer canoes were in use by the French by 1670.

Baron de La Hontan made interesting observations of birchbark canoes at Montréal in 1684. He had seen a hundred large and small canoes, but he thought that the French would have use only for the large ones for trade. He said that the Indians used mostly the small ones, and they sat in these on their heels, though he noted that at the slightest movement these little canoes would turn over. (He did not realize that most Indians who used the birchbark canoe went their entire lives without turning over in one.)

The original Algonquin canoes were rarely longer than 6 m (20 ft.). The great canoes of the fur trade came into being because of the need to transport large amounts of merchandise great distances to Lake Superior and beyond and to return to Montréal with prodigious amounts of furs. The French authorities at one point regulated the number of canoes that could be used in the fur trade, so this also tended to increase the canoes' length. Indians (quite possibly Algonquin) at first made the larger canoes to order and later under the supervision of the French. After a time, French craftsmen also worked on their construction. Fur trade canoe factories were established at Trois-Rivières, downstream from Montréal, and elsewhere. The Algonquin sometimes worked in these factories, as did Indians of other tribes, and there was also a very active trade in rolls of birch bark for canoe manufacture.

In the 1750s Col. Louis Franquet reported that the factories at Trois-Rivières made canoes of a standard model, 10 m (33 ft.) in length, 1.5 m (5 ft.) in the beam, and 75 cm (30 in.) deep. They made twenty canoes per year. After construction at Trois-Rivières, the canoes were sent to Montréal, the eastern terminus of the fur trade. Algonquin were regular traders at French settlements, and Trois-Rivières had a permanent settlement of Algonquin. Eastern Indians also were employed to build canoes in western areas. To what extent Algonquin may have done so is not known, but the Montréal Merchants Records may hold some information.

When the English obtained control of New France in 1763, they also took over much of the fur trade. The great birchbark canoes remained the backbone of commerce. In one government storehouse, the English discovered six thousand cords of birch bark for canoes.

Whether the Algonquin were the last to make the great fur trade canoes to any great extent is not certain, but they may well have been. These large, striking canoes were made by the Algonquin in western Québec even as late as the beginning of the twentieth century. Adney, in the only detailed description we have, documents fur trade canoe construction by Algonquin under the supervision of Louis A. Christopherson, Hudson's Bay Company factor (post manager) at Grand Lake Victoria and for a time Lac Barrière. Adney records that an Algonquin master builder from Maniwaki worked for a time as a canoe maker for Christopherson. The father of present-day canoe builder Jim Jerome constructed fur trade canoes at Lac Andostagan and then paddled the canoes to Lac Barrière, a day's voyage

In this photograph taken in western Québec around the turn of the century, L. A. Christopherson faces starboard, fourth from right. The long dark beard of the priest was typical of the Oblate missionaries of western Québec during this period. (Photo courtesy Édmond Brouillard, O.M.I., Lac Simon, Québec.)

north, where they were purchased by the factor, perhaps some of the time by Christopherson.

Toward the end of the nineteenth century, Christopherson paid an Indian master builder $45 for making a fur trade canoe. Christopherson supplied the materials, which he got from Indians in trade, and paid women to do the sewing. The total cost for a large canoe was about $100. In that day, this was not a small sum. One missionary, responsible for Grand Lake Victoria among other missions, wrote to his bishop in 1889 that receipts from various missions, including Grand Lake Victoria, totaled $23, which, according to him, was an "insufficient sum for becoming rich." The yearly compensation of an Oblate missionary at the time was on the order of $250 or $300.

Christopherson told Adney:

The widths of the five-fathom canoe varied according to whether the canoe was intended for speed or for cargo capacity. Ours were built for speed, the carrying of valuable cargo between Lake Victoria and Mattawa. Their width was about four feet with a capacity of two and a half tons of cargo, in addition to a crew of six men with their equipment and provisions. On the portages, the canoe was carried by four men, two under each end, the canoe being bottom up. Some carried it by two men in front and only one behind but that was dangerous, for if the man slipped, the canoe, in falling, might cripple him seriously. I knew one man who had an accident of that kind and had thereafter to go on crutches. I preferred Indian canoemen to white men. Indians were more cautious and careful and with a large canoe carrying valuable cargo, prudence was of the first importance.

During thirty years, I never had but one accident. This occurred when shooting a timber-chute. The leading canoe struck an iron spike which the winter's frost had drawn out and it tore a bad hole in her bottom.

Grand Lake Victoria, Lac Barrière, Kipawa, and Lake Abititi were the areas in which fur trade canoes were built around the upper Ottawa River in the period after 1880.

Well into the twentieth century, Europeans came in some cases to depend on birchbark

This canoe, now owned by the Buffalo Canoe Club and stored on Lake Erie near Ridgeway, Ontario, is said to be the longest birchbark canoe in existence. Apparently crafted by the Algonquin along the lower Ottawa River around 1860, the canoe is 24 ft., 9 in. long, weighs 220 pounds, and has an outer beam of 52 1/2 in., an inner beam of 48 1/2 in., and a depth of 19 1/2 in. A single sheet of bark was used along the bottom; the lettering was done with natural dyes. (Photo courtesy Richard Nash.)

A Hudson's Bay Company canoe from Grand Lake Victoria arrives at Kipawa in June 1902, loaded with the season's furs for shipment to Montréal. The rolls of bark were intended for canoe building and would be shipped to posts where bark could not be found. (Photo courtesy Archives of Ontario, Charles Macnamara.)

canoes almost as much as the Indians, not only in the fur trade, but also for hunting, fishing, and travel. In the nineteenth and twentieth centuries in western Québec, non-natives sometimes took up the craft of birchbark canoe building.

Determining the traditional Algonquin model is difficult. In the Maniwaki and Rapid Lake areas, the old model is called *rabeska* by some of the living builders. It is said that the Algonquin name for the large fur trade canoes was *nabiska*. Adney says that the name *rabeska*, rather than the French *maître canot*, was long applied by the white men in the fur trade to the large canoes built for their business in the Ottawa River Valley.

The old-style Algonquin canoe had a rather narrow beam, flaring sides, and a fairly sharp bow. The sheer was straight over the middle, rose slightly toward the ends, and went up perpendicularly at the bow. This bow feature distinguished it from the newer Algonquin model, the *wábanäki tcîmân*.

The bottom of the old model was gently rounded, flatter than is found in the canoes of most other tribes. (Flat bottoms generally offer more stability.) The stem curved up at the water level, went straight for most of its length, and then bent sharply back to join the outwales and the gunwale cover, sometimes descending and sometimes going straight back as it joined them. There is a strong resemblance between the *rabeska* stem configuration and the basic fur trade canoe bow.

Adney made a model of an Algonquin old-style canoe, which he called "one of the most beautiful of the birch canoes." It is now in the collection of The Mariners' Museum. It is a 1:5 model 82 cm (32 in.) long, 17 cm (6¾ in.) in outer beam, and 6.5 cm (2½ in.) in depth.

It was fashioned after an old-style canoe depicted in *The Bark Canoes and Skin Boats of North America* (page 113), which had been made by Tommy Sarazin, then of Golden Lake but formerly of Maniwaki. Adney describes the *rabeska* as the "natural" canoe of the Algonquin.

By the late nineteenth century, sportsmen were using birchbark canoes extensively. They were probably the most easily procured canoes at the time, particularly in western Québec and eastern Ontario. Some of the major suppliers were the Indians of St. François du Lac, on the south shore of the St. Lawrence between Montréal and Québec. Nicolas Panadis, an Abnaki builder from there, reported that he and a partner (probably with the help of their wives and others) in one year built thirty canoes for the Montréal market. These canoes probably averaged less than 5 m (16 ft.) in length.

At the end of the nineteenth century, the Canadian Pacific Railway was built through Mattawa, Ontario, east of Ottawa and in the heart of the Algonquin territory not far from Golden Lake. This opened up prime hunting and fishing territory for sportsmen. Mattawa was, at the time, a little lumbering town on the Ottawa River. Most of the canoes there were small (4 to 4.5 m long) and for the use of fishermen and big-game hunters. But there still would have been some large canoes there, as Mattawa was at the end of the railway line from which point trade canoes still departed to James Bay and Hudson Bay.

Colin Rankin, the Hudson's Bay Company factor at Mattawa, outfitted sportsmen and provided guides from the local Algonquin. Rankin kept birchbark canoes in a canoe shed behind the post. It is likely he would have obtained these from Montréal, where the post

An old-style model of an Algonquin canoe from the Ottawa River area, 1861. (Photo courtesy Museum of Mankind, London.)

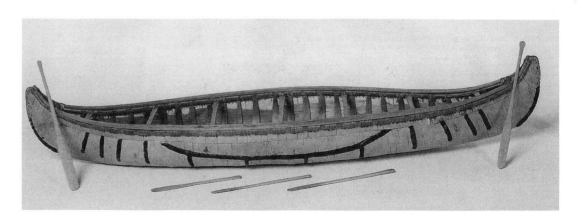

would have acquired the rest of its furnishings for sportsmen. The canoes possibly came from the Abnaki at St. François du Lac. The post also had the larger fur trade canoes, as it was a departure point for trading voyages into the hinterland and to James Bay.

The Abnaki, to the east of the Algonquin territory, had a major influence on the Algonquin canoe form. Such was the influx and influence of the Abnaki canoe into the lower Ottawa Valley that by the year 1900 the Algonquin at Golden Lake and at Maniwaki had adopted the eastern style of canoe, which they called the *wâbanäki tcîmân*, as their most common model. Today the old-style Algonquin canoe is rarely seen, and when it is made it tends to be less than faithful to the traditional workmanship. One of the last builders of the old-style Algonquin canoe, around 1900, was Tommy Sarazin of Golden Lake, who was born in Maniwaki.

In adopting the Abnaki canoe form, the Algonquin nevertheless did retain features of their old canoe style. The headboard of the Abnaki canoe is thin and bellied toward the bow, but the Algonquin originally made the *wâbanäki tcîmân* with a thick, vertical headboard braced by a longitudinal strut to the stem-piece, and with the headboard and stempiece joined outside the canoe and placed together in the bow. More recent ways of making this canoe eliminate one or more of these steps, however.

The importance of the canoe to the Algonquin way of life up through the nineteenth century cannot be understated. Language books were often written with an attempt to involve the culture in teaching the language. When the French missionaries did this in books on the Algonquin language, they gave an intriguing glimpse into the life of the people. In the following sentences, part of a drill in conversation from an 1891 missionary grammar (Abbé Cuoq's *Grammaire de la langue algonquine*), it is clear how great a part the canoe played in the scheme of things:

You're good at making canoes. Hurry up and make one.

That's what I intend to do. I have bark for a canoe, good bark.

I only need a small canoe for myself.

I'll make you one then. How long do you need it?

Ten feet will be good enough.

Here is your canoe. Do you like it?

Yes, I like it. But it is not yet gummed.

I'll gum it tomorrow.

The waves are dangerous. Water is coming in the canoe. There is a small island over there. Let's try to get to it.

Let's make a fire before it rains.

Pull the canoe farther up on the shore so the wind doesn't take it away.

Do you think the wind will stop us for long?

Tomorrow the wind may go down and we may be able to leave.

In Algonquin territory around the turn of the century, the increasing use of canvas canoes was one of the major factors in the decline in

White hunters with an old-style Algonquin canoe and two wâbanäki tcîmân *models in western Québec, circa 1900. (Photo courtesy Mulligan Collection.)*

Abitibi, western Québec, around 1910. (Photo courtesy Édmond Brouillard, O.M.I., Lac Simon Québec.)

Indians portaging canoes and tourists carrying loads with tumplines, circa 1920. (Photo courtesy Désert Lake Fish and Game Club.)

White fishermen with Algonquin guides from Maniwaki in western Québec in the 1920s. The two canoes are lashed together with poles across the intermediate thwarts. (Photo courtesy Désert Lake Fish and Game Club.)

Xavier Commanda from Maniwaki poses with a tourist in a canvas canoe in the 1920s. (Photo courtesy Désert Lake Fish and Game Club.)

A River Désert Indian displaying a fine canoe at Désert Lake in the 1920s. (Photo courtesy Désert Lake Fish and Game Club.)

Gumming a canoe at Golden Lake, Ontario, 1927. (Photo courtesy Museum of the American Indian, Heye Foundation.)

the manufacture and use of the birchbark canoe. Birchbark canoes were, however, still used by white sportsmen and by Indians for hunting, trapping, and transportation. The Algonquin continued to make them until late in the twentieth century at Golden Lake in Ontario and Maniwaki (River Désert) and Rapid Lake (Lac Barrière) in Québec. There is very little information on birchbark canoe making elsewhere, but these canoes undoubtedly were built after the turn of the century at other Algonquin locations in Québec, such as Lac Simon, Pikogan, and Kipawa.

Adney points out a development that had taken place since the turn of the century. The price of furs had been relatively good, and the Indian builder could, with the effort of a day or two of trapping, earn enough to buy a factory-made canvas canoe. Because of this, many builders ceased making birchbark canoes for themselves or for sale.

Yvon Couture, in his book *Les Algonquins,* describes life at Hunter's Point in the 1930s. The Algonquin there subsisted almost exclusively from hunting and fishing, though on occasion a man would work as a guide, lumberjack, or fire warden. The government annually furnished wood, flannel blankets, and rubber boots to each family. If a man was sick and unable to support his family, the family received $22 a month. The Algonquin lived in log cabins and fashioned their own furniture from wood. The men made birchbark canoes, and they traveled by canoe in summer and by dogsled in winter. Couture says that in 1983 the remains of old birchbark canoes could still be found behind buildings at Winneway and Hunter's Point.

GOLDEN LAKE, ONTARIO

In the 1830s the Hudson's Bay Company established a post at Golden Lake, Ontario, to trade with area Algonquin. The main supply route at the time was by canoe from Lac des Deux Montagnes (Oka) near Montréal, up the Ottawa River, and then up the Bonnechère River to Golden Lake.

Birchbark canoes continued to be manufactured in Golden Lake right up until 1994. Throughout the twentieth century, there were several well-known and skilled Algonquin builders on the reserve.

Adney collected a substantial amount of information at Golden Lake Reserve in the 1920s. A photo by Adney in *The Bark Canoes and Skin Boats of North America* (page 120) shows the wife and children of canoe maker Dan Sarazin in a *wâbanäki tcîmân* built by Golden Lake builder Tommy Sarazin. Tommy Sarazin was one of the last skilled builders of the Algonquin old-style canoe.

In the 1920s Basil Patridge built canoes at Golden Lake, making several *wâbanäki tcîmân* type canoes each year. Some said he was the best canoe builder at the time; others said Tommy Sarazin was.

Other twentieth-century Golden Lake canoe builders included Vincent Mikans, Joe Jocko, Dave Kokoko, Lamab Sarazin, and Jumbo Tenasco.

During the time of Tommy Sarazin and after, one of the best-known builders was Matt Bernard. An excellent 1942 documentary shows Matt making a canoe about 18 feet long. It is a *wâbanäki tcîmân* and quite well made. The gunwales appear to be made with black ash rather than spruce. The film follows Matt and his wife as they collect natural spruce gum for sealing the canoe, boil it, and take out the impurities. Then Matt's wife works it into a taffylike mass. In one of the most enjoyable sequences in any birchbark canoe-making film, the completed canoe is taken by four men on a rigorous trip through rapids. This film clearly shows how good a birchbark canoe maker Matt Bernard was.

Dan Sarazin, whose work is highlighted in Chapter VI, was active for decades in birchbark canoe making. He died in the early 1980s. He constructed many canoes as exhibitions and was a highly skilled craftsman. A particularly fine example of his work is a kind of cross

An old-style Algonquin canoe built by Tommy Sarazin, who was born in Maniwâki. This photograph was taken at Golden Lake in the 1920s. (Photo courtesy The Mariners' Museum, E. T. Adney.)

Master canoe builder Lamab Sarazin, Golden Lake Algonquin and the father of Dan Sarazin, works a hide over a tcicakosidjigan. (Photo courtesy The Mariners' Museum, E. T. Adney.)

Dan Sarazin's wife and children at Golden Lake in the 1920s. The canoe, a wâbanäki tcîmân, was made by Dan's uncle, Tommy Sarazin. (Photo courtesy The Mariners' Museum. E. T. Adney.)

Dan Sarazin's son Stanley at Golden Lake, Ontario, in May 1991. The shop in the background is where Stanley makes his canoes, including this 14-foot model that was made with a single sheet of bark. (Photo by David Gidmark.)

A Stanley Sarazin canoe under construction, Golden Lake, May 1991. (Photo by David Gidmark.)

Pete Dubé of Maniwaki, 1929. Dubé, born in Manouan, was a master birchbark canoe builder, and also made paddles inlaid with bone. (Photo courtesy Museum of the American Indian, Heye Foundation.)

Charlie Commanda, perhaps the most skilled builder at River Désert in this century. (Photo courtesy Museum of the American Indian, Heye Foundation.)

section of a *wâbanäki tcîmân* under construction at Ste.-Marie Among the Hurons in Midland, Ontario.

Dan's son, Stanley, has continued in birchbark canoe construction. He is a skilled builder and makes his canoes with much the same rib work, spruce root work, and gunwale structure as his father's. He made a canoe as recently as spring 1994, at which time he was 56 years old. Though Stanley has given a number of birchbark canoe-building courses on the reserve, no younger builders are now making birchbark canoes.

Another Golden Lake resident intermittently active in canoe making is Percy Commanda, 67 years old in 1994. He started building in 1972. He spent three summers at Canoe Lake in Algonquin Park building birchbark canoes, several of which ended up in England and Germany. A film was made of Percy Commanda in 1974.

MANIWAKI (RIVER DÉSERT), QUÉBEC

At Maniwaki, birchbark canoes have been built throughout the twentieth century, though since 1990 only four have been made. These canoes were constructed by Basil Smith, who was eighty-three in 1994. The Maniwaki canoes have varied in construction from superb to next to egregious in craftsmanship, the latter being the products of more recent builders.

One excellent Maniwaki builder in the earlier part of this century was Charlie Commanda, whose superb workmanship can be seen in an old-style Algonquin canoe now at Désert Lake Fish and Game Club, about 70 km (40 mi.) northwest of Maniwaki. The canoe has finely carved ribs and careful root work. From center thwart to bows, the ribs are tapered in thickness and width and the spruce root becomes finer. Charlie Commanda's work is a good indication of the fine craftsmen who existed at Maniwaki not long ago.

Canoe builders who were active at Maniwaki during the twentieth century include John Carle and his sons Jocko and Peter; William Commanda; Pete Dubé and his son Jean; Paddy Chausée; Joe Groulx; Jocko John Bull; Joe Cooko; Patrick Tolley (who lived north of Maniwaki and brought his canoes down to sell them to buy food); Simon Cayer; Clément Jocko; Antoine

Jocko; Xavier Twenish; Antoine St. Denis; and Madenine Clément.

One Maniwaki canoe maker, Jocko Carle, resumed birchbark canoe building in 1979 after a hiatus of thirty-seven years. He most often built canoes with his trapping partner of fifty-five years, Basil Smith. After Jocko's death in 1981, Basil Smith continued to build birchbark canoes on his own, and on occasion with the author.

The Poirier General Store in Maniwaki, started by Joseph Poirier in 1911, sold full-size birchbark canoes for decades. Most of the canoes that were sold were 14 or 15 feet long. In the early years, Poirier would purchase them for $1 a foot and sell them for $1.25 a foot. Most of these early canoes came from the Indians near Maniwaki.

Just after the turn of the century, there weren't a lot of tourists in the Maniwaki area, so the birchbark canoe trade was not great. Many of the local people who used them bought them directly from the Indians. In the 1940s canoe sales were greater. Sometimes the store would have as many as twenty over the winter, which they kept in a shed behind the store. In the spring, cracks from the cold weather would have to be sealed up by passing a hot iron over the gum. For the canoes sold at Poirier's, the Indian builders usually used spruce root and wooden pegs. If a canoe sold by Poirier needed repair, Poirier would arrange for it with the Indian builder.

GRAND LAKE VICTORIA, QUÉBEC

There were about three hundred people at Grand Lake Victoria around 1800. In the nineteenth century, Hudson's Bay Company established a post there and the Oblates maintained a church. Around 1900 it was the center for festivals for Indians from Lac Barrière, Lac-à-la-Truite, Harricana, and Nottaway. By 1929 the population was down to eighty-five, mainly because of infectious diseases.

The importance of the canoe to the natives here can be seen in more than one way. They fished, hunted, and trapped using birchbark canoes. The Grand Lake Victoria Indians would go a long way to follow a watercourse rather than crossing a height of land to get to a given destination.

In the 1970s the local canoe builders made

The Poirier General Store in Maniwaki, Québec, 1940. The sign at left advertises "Reliable Guides" and "Birch Bark Canoes For Sale." Many of the canoes were crafted by Patrick Maranda, David Makakons, and Paul Matchewan from Lac Barrière. (Photo courtesy Claire Poirier.)

River Désert Algonquin Sam Commanda and a white fisherman in a birchbark canoe in western Québec in the 1920s. (Photo courtesy Désert Lake Fish and Game Club.)

canvas canoes, although they were still able to build birchbark ones. Twentieth-century Grand Lake Victoria canoe makers include Frank Penosway, Jean-Paul Anichinapeo, and Sam Moïse.

The post journals from Grand Lake Victoria give an idea of the important part played by birchbark canoes, both the big trade canoes and the smaller family canoes, in the daily activities of the post.

From the Grand Lake Victoria post journal for 1883:

May 19. Braseau and boy Pierre and Kawisitch arrived this evening. Mr. Main and Edward busy making preparation to start off a big canoe to Dumoine.

May 27. Antisokan and band arrived this morning. Started a big canoe for Dumoine this evening, Mr. Main in charge. Started off the Barrière packet this evening—two men in a small canoe.

And from factor Louis Christopherson's Grand Lake Victoria journal of 1892:

May 9. An Indian was gumming a canoe and knocking timbers in. [These "timbers" were canoe ribs. This would have been the spring refurbishing of the canoe. Ribs would have been knocked a few inches toward the center thwart to reduce chances of the bark's cracking under rib pressure during the dry winter months.]

May 26. One canoe left this morning for Bay Lake.

May 27. Canoe arrived back from Bay Lake. Christopherson and clerk opened all boxes. Forbes [a clerk] and Nottaway [a Barrière Indian] arrived from Barrière.

June 1. Christopherson and Forbes and Indians packed all furs. Old chief came in today and paid his account. Braseau arrived and brought in three bears. No sign of canoe from Bay Lake.

June 2. The canoe arrived early this morning. Forbes marking packs. Christopherson in store working at books.

June 5. Canoes arrived back from Bay Lake. Wescatia is watching flour as a few boxes got wet in canoes.

June 6. Christopherson and Forbes in the store getting five crews to go to Bay Lake in the morning.

June 8. The big canoes arrived this afternoon.

June 11. A beautiful day. Christopherson, Edward and Forbes all busy attending the Indians in the store. The canoes were all gummed and ready for the station.

June 13. Mr. Christopherson, Mr. Edward and Mr. MacKenzie started at half-past 4 o'clock this morning with returns of five big canoes down to the station.

June 16. The fur canoes are having rainy weather.

June 25. Wind north. A fine day. Mr. Christopherson and brigade arrived at about 9 this morning and glad to say they are all well. They were busy opening out the boxes.

July 6. Started off big canoe to Dumoine for the government flour this morning.

July 20. Forbes and his wife arrived from Barrière this evening. They brought down a young heifer in the big canoe.

July 23. The Barrière canoe started off early this morning.

July 25. Mr. Christopherson and crew of five men started off for Mattawa about 4 o'clock this morning.

August 5. How glad I was to see the canoe this morning arriving from Mattawa. I am glad to say that Mr. Christopherson arrived in good health.

Sadly, birchbark canoes are no longer made at Grand Lake Victoria, and have not been for decades.

LAC BARRIÈRE (RAPID LAKE), QUÉBEC

Lac Barrière had always been isolated. Before a road was built through Barrière territory, all goods came by canoe from Mattawa via Grand Lake Victoria. Usually only men traveled in this commerce.

Into the 1920s the Barrière Indians would travel by birchbark canoe down to Maniwaki, 160 km (100 mi.) away, and would also make long canoe trips to trade furs at North Bay, Ontario, over 320 km (200 mi.) distant. In the

A gathering of canoes at the Hudson's Bay Company post in Grand Lake Victoria, Québec, on Procession Sunday 1895. At least two of the canoes (see upper left) are large rabeskas. (Photo courtesy National Museums of Canada, L. A. Christopherson.)

A fur trade canoe brigade near Grand Lake Victoria in 1885. Louis Christopherson is in the white shirt and flat cap, sitting with his hands crossed. (Photo courtesy Smithsonian Institution.)

The Hudson's Bay Company post at Grand Lake Victoria, circa 1942. (Photo courtesy Hudson's Bay Company Archives.)

late 1920s, anthropologist Frederick Johnson visited Lac Barrière and wrote about the settlement at the time.

The settlement was then composed of twenty-five families. The chief was David Makakons, who had been a canoe maker all his life. In those days, the authority of the chief was more or less limited to the time the band was in the summer settlement, with the band dispersed for most of the cold months to the hunting territories where families spent as much as three-quarters of the year. By the late 1920s, many birchbark canoes were still in use, but there were already some canvas canoes with motors rigged to them.

According to Jacob Wawatie, who had lived at Barrière, a master canoe maker would make a birchbark canoe with a boy of fourteen or fifteen. Then he would take the boy, along with materials for a second canoe, to an island. He'd tell the boy to go into the woods to look for spruce root. When the boy did so, the master would depart, leaving provisions behind. The only way the boy could leave the island was to make a serviceable canoe.

Twentieth-century Barrière builders included Michel Maranda; Sévère Nanish (according to some, one of the best); Noë Maranda; brothers Paul and Louis Matchewan; Daniel Kee; Abraham Ratt; father Moïse Ratt; Noël Jerome; Benjamin Jocko; John Jerome; Michel Toske; Frank Toske; George Jerome; and Basil Decourcy. Those who have made a birchbark canoe since 1980 are Jim Jerome, John Ratt, Alec Ratt, Lina Nottaway, and Albert Poucachiche.

George Jerome (Jim Jerome's uncle) and George's wife at Lac Barrière in 1929. (Photo courtesy Museum of the American Indian, Heye Foundation.)

The canoe still retains importance at Lac Barrière: Angus Nottaway with his dog, trapping gear, washboard, and snowmobile in a canvas canoe on his way to the trapline, November 1989. (Photo by David Gidmark.)

One birchbark canoe builder, Isaac Jerome, used to leave as many as fifteen canoes at various places in the woods so that the family wouldn't have to portage all the time. He would tell the children to take a gum pot with them when they went to use one of the canoes.

Alec Ratt and his wife at Lac Barrière in 1985. (Photo by David Gidmark.)

Lina Nottaway returning from raising a fish net at Nanawatan, near Lac Barrière, in 1991. (Photo by David Gidmark.)

Perhaps the best known of the Lac Barrière builders of the twentieth century was Patrick Maranda. His band was known fore its excellent canoe-making craftsmen, of whom he was reputed to be the most skilled. His canoes are characterized by a very elegant sheer and fairly straight rocker, along with fine crooked knife work on the ribs and sheathing.

David Makakons was another skilled builder of birchbark canoes in the twentieth century. He always used them, though if he happened to be caught somewhere without his birchbark canoe, he would use a canvas canoe--but only then. Behind his cabin, he had a little shed as a workshop, where he kept neatly carved paddles, ribs, rolls of good birch bark, a wooden spud for peeling bark from trees, awls, and a crooked knife. David and Michel Toske, another old birchbark canoe builder, often sat on the porch and shouted jokes at each other: both were nearly deaf.

On a visit to Rapid Lake in 1984, I saw a 4-foot model birchbark canoe made by Lina Nottaway. It was made of good bark, had the general Barrière sheer and rocker, had attractive spruce root lashing on the gunwales, and was obviously done by someone skilled with a crooked knife, for the cedar ribs and sheathing were well done.

The skills of birchbark canoe making survive among the Barrière builders, although there has been little activity in birchbark canoe making there in recent years because of the canoe makers' employment as hunting and fishing guides, their work for lumber companies, and the fact that canvas and synthetic canoes have mostly replaced birchbark embarkations.

There are a number of reasons for the decline in more recent times in the production

of birchbark canoes among the Algonquin. Despite the ubiquity of synthetic canoes, prices of birchbark canoes have risen considerably in recent years. The canoe makers are old now, and relief from their posts of service is slow in coming, if ever.

Another reason for the decline in birchbark canoes is that good canoe bark is becoming increasingly harder to find. In the mid-1950s Matt Bernard and his helpers traveled 1,000 miles to locate canoe bark for the 11-meter (36-ft.) canoe they were building. In 1989 I traveled 600 miles to find suitable bark for a canoe Jim Jerome was building.

One explanation for the shortage of bark large enough and of good enough quality for a birchbark canoe comes from D. S. Davidson's article "Folk Tales from Grand Lake Victoria, Québec." On a visit there in 1926, Davidson heard a story about a mythological being named Meso, who was able to talk the language of all things, animate and inanimate as well.

When the Indians first learned to use birch bark for canoes and utensils, Meso foresaw the possibility of the Indian utilizing all the trees in the forest. He was afraid that if good building bark could be found

David Makakons displaying his building bed, building frame, and a roll of bark at Lac Barrière in 1929. (Photo courtesy Museum of the American Indian, Heye Foundation.)

on every birch tree, the Indians would become extravagant and would not take care of the things they made. He feared the Indians would throw things away while they were still useful and that they would make no effort to find those which had become lost. It appeared to him that the Indians would never become thrifty as long as there was a good supply of bark on every tree. All the trees would soon be cut down and that would mean the end of the forest upon which the Indians and the game were dependent for so much. Meso, therefore, climbed into many of the birch trees and swayed them about until their trunks became crooked and twisted. This he did to protect the forest. He also took a balsam bough and switched many of the trees. He scarred many of them so much that it is now difficult to find one which will yield a suitable piece of bark large enough to make even a birchbark box.

Mrs. David Makakons with her two-day-old baby in a tikinâgan at Lac Barrière in 1929. To the right, David Makakons carves ribs for a canoe. (Photo courtesy Museum of the American Indian, Heye Foundation.)

David Makakons, the long-time chief at Lac Barrière, with one of his birchbark canoes. On the left is Charlie Smith, River Désert Algonquin and the father of Mary Commanda. When this photo was taken in 1959, David was in his eighties and still making birchbark canoes. The wooden deck-pieces visible in the canoe were typical of David's work but unusual in most other canoes. (Photo courtesy Leonard Lee Rue III.)

II

General Construction Techniques

MATERIALS

Birch Bark

Birch bark for canoes comes from the white birch (*Betula papyrifera* Marshall), also known as the canoe birch or paper birch. The Algonquin canoe makers distinguish between canoe and paper birch, although to the layman's eye all white birches look much the same. The canoe maker rejects bark that layers easily and looks too "papery" in favor of solid-looking bark, which often has a silver tinge to it. So when the builder uses the term paper birch, he is referring to bark that will likely be unacceptable. Some builders say that good bark has green moss on it.

All of Canada and the continental United States have at least some birch. In the usual generosity of nature, birch bark suitable for canoes is commonly found, across the continent, in areas where canoes are most needed. The upper limit of the heavily deciduous forest is reached above Maniwaki, Québec. Beyond that, pine, spruce, and other conifers predominate. For this reason, Rapid Lake and Manouan, in western Québec, have continued to be centers for canoe building. In the southern and western states, the birch populations are in no way as significant as in the northern parts of the continent.

A canoe birch. (Photo by David Gidmark.)

Birch grows in various sites but prefers moist, rich soil. The large white birch is often scattered among coniferous or northern deciduous trees. In western Québec, some of the builders look for the best trees on hills along with hardwoods such as maple and yellow birch. Other builders feel that the best birches for canoes are found on lower-lying areas and say that birches high up on hills tend to be too dry.

Birch bark is impervious to water and is durable in part because of a resin called betulin. The pliability of birch bark is amazing. A birchbark canoe can go through rapids that would damage a wood-and-canvas canoe. The bark and hand-split sheathing and ribs are more flexible than the comparable members of a wood-and-canvas canoe. Lina Nottaway of Barrière Lake has noted that a bark canoe is stronger than a canvas canoe; when canvas is scratched, a hole is made, but not so with birch bark.

Only the outer bark layer is removed for use in canoes, while the inner, pulpy layer of bark, called the cambium, remains on the tree.

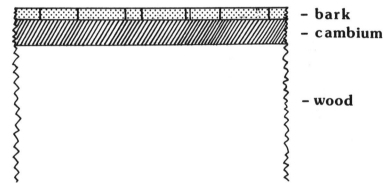

– **bark**

– **cambium**

– **wood**

A birch tree in cross section.

Bark is most often harvested during the summer months, as that is when it is easiest to peel from the tree. Winter bark was prized by the Algonquin, however. Some builders believed it was stronger than summer bark. Also, designs could be scraped on canoes made of winter bark. Winter bark retains a dark inner layer, which can be scraped away to leave the dark designs. Winter bark may occur as late as May or June or as early as September. Sometimes a canoe was made with the main sheet of the lighter summer bark, but winter bark for the side pieces. The builder could then make designs on the sides.

There can be as many as thirty layers in a single thickness of the outer bark of birch bark. Lenticels, commonly known as "eyes," are horizontal pores in the bark that allow respiration. The rest of the bark is airtight, and all of the bark, including the eyes, is watertight.

In poor bark, however, eyes can open up. This is an important test that the bark must pass for use in canoe making.

When looking for bark, the Algonquin builder usually would return to the site where he previously got canoe bark, confident that he stood a good chance of finding a suitable large sheet of bark nearby. In the previous two decades, a builder from Maniwaki or Rapid Lake usually could go into the woods and come back with a suitable sheet of bark the same day. Within the last five or ten years, though, this is becoming more difficult, and it might take several days to locate suitable bark. Large birches are still easy to find; large birches with healthy bark of quality are not. Their bark seems to be drier than before, and the eyes open up more easily. Acid rain may possibly be the cause of this deterioration in quality. Smaller trees, with sheets 75 cm (30 in.) wide or less, seem to have healthy bark, though the sheets are too small for full-size canoes.

To locate a tree today, most of the builders drive along the bush roads in a truck until they come to a location they know to have large birches. Tops of birches often can be sighted from the road. Then the builder walks back to the tree to see if it is suitable for a canoe.

The tree must be straight and without knots for about 4.5 m (15 ft.) to make a canoe of 4 m (13 ft.). The bottom meter (3 ft.) of the trunk usually has fairly rough bark, so the 4.5-m (15-ft.) sheet must be taken above this.

The bark must be tested in the good section, not in the rough area. It is tested by cutting with an ax down to the cambium layer. Then a sample from 10 to 15 cm is removed. Often this sample is taken from the entire circumference of the tree, so that the width of the potential sheet can be measured. This enables the builder to calculate quickly whether he will need to add side pieces to the main sheet of bark.

The bark sample is bent back on itself to see if it cracks or delaminates, qualities not desirable in canoe bark. Then it is bent in the other direction to see if the eyes open up. In dry or sick bark, these eyes open up readily; such bark is not harvested. In general, the canoe builder looks for bark with eyes that are short and widely spaced, rather than long and close together. If the eyes are too long, Lina Nottaway points out, the bark sheet could split across the canoe bottom from gunwale to gunwale. Also, bark with short eyes is easier to peel from the tree.

Pliability is the most important factor in selecting birch bark for a canoe. Thin bark of good pliability can be used for a canoe, whereas very thick bark that is not pliable but is otherwise healthy should not.

The importance of a large sheet of good-quality birch bark to the construction of a canoe cannot be overemphasized. Even a skilled builder would make an unacceptable canoe if the bark sheet were of poor quality.

Once the builder has determined that the bark is of sufficient quality, the tree is cut down. Currently this is done with a chain saw although, as Jim Jerome notes, the trees were formerly cut down with bucksaws or axes. Full-size sheets usually were not taken while the tree was still standing. Some builders, such as Dan Sarazin of Golden Lake, occasionally took bark this way. Dan's son, Stanley, does not favor this method because he feels it wastes trees.

There are several problems in taking a bark sheet from a standing tree. The first is that a ladder must be made in the woods or carried in. Second, the ladder usually must be supported against the trunk of the tree from which the sheet is to be taken, which means it is leaning against the bark sheet, making the difficult task of removing the bark sheet even more so. And removing bark from a tree that is standing risks ruining the sheet by buckling.

The part of the birch trunk that will yield the bark sheet must be kept off the ground as the tree falls, so that it does not hit rocks and stumps on the ground, causing damage to the bark sheet. The tree's own branches usually keep the top end off the ground, while the bottom end of the trunk near the stump is held off by a heavy solid log that the builder places crossways where the end of the trunk will fall. If the builder can keep that end of the trunk off the ground, he can usually be confident that the whole clear part of the trunk will remain off the ground, though sometimes the trunk's weight and momentum will cause it to jump off the support. If the builder is able to remove an intact sheet in that case, he is very fortunate.

Once the trunk is resting on the support, a straight line is cut along the top of the trunk, usually using a chain saw. Occasionally there is an advantage to cutting this straight line along the side of the trunk instead. This is most often done if there is a knot or blemish on the bark. Then the straight line can pass through the blemish and the maximum width of the sheet can be achieved.

After the longitudinal cut is made in the birch trunk, the peeling of the bark begins. The blade of an ax is wedged under the outer layer of bark, perhaps slightly into the cambium. The bark is peeled away, and the builder can soon see how easy it is going to be to peel the sheet on this particular day. The bark sheet must be peeled evenly. It may be peeled only 2 cm (1 in.) at a time or so before advancing the entire length of the trunk. Getting too much ahead at one end or the other risks tearing the sheet. Good birch bark is very hard to cut across the eyes, but it can be cut or ripped easily along the eyes.

In a canoe, supported by the ribs and sheathing, birch bark is very strong. But from the peeling stage to the finished canoe, the bark can be damaged. In one case, a roll of bark was ripped as it caught a thick branch while being taken from the woods. In another case, a builder was clearing branches from beneath a fallen trunk so that it would be easier to remove the bark sheet, and he put the ax through the bark.

As the bark starts to come off, sticking points are often reached. Care must be taken, usually with the ax blade, to work the bark beyond those points. Sometimes spuds are used as aids in peeling. These can be wooden wedges or pieces of thick birch bark perhaps 20 cm (8 in.) wide. To help bring the bark sheet off evenly over a long stretch, the builder often cuts a sapling 2 m (6 ft.) or longer. He and his helper then push this evenly and carefully between the bark sheet and the cambium layer. They do this up and down the trunk and are very careful to watch for sticking points. Even with the distributed pressure provided by the sapling, the bark could be torn at a sticking point.

When the bark sheet is finally removed, it is first laid on the ground white side down. Then the workers carefully turn it over, white side up, and lay it on a flat piece of ground next to the tree or, if there is none, on the trunk itself. If the sun is shining, they try to lay it in the sun for ten or fifteen minutes to warm the bark and make it easier and less risky to roll.

Then, two people roll the bark carefully, white side in. While one rolls the bark, the other carefully feeds the sheet flat into the roll. When the rolling is finished, the roll is tied at both ends so that it can be carried from the woods. Occasionally it is tied with a tumpline, and then the tumpline is put around the forehead and the roll is carried from the woods. Poor-quality bark usually will not make it to the stage where it can be rolled up and carried from the woods.

The bark is kept in the roll until it is used. It can be kept for several years before use. If it is kept a long time, it must be soaked in water before it is unrolled on the building bed. Sometimes a builder will use a fresh roll without immersing it in water, but most often, even if the roll is relatively fresh, it is soaked in water for a few days.

With a finished canoe, in order to help preserve the bark, the ribs sometimes were knocked about 5 cm (2 in.) inboard from the vertical for winter storage. This reduced pressure on the bark, making it less likely to split. The split that occurred most often was from gunwale to gunwale at the center thwart. This can often be seen in museum canoes, particularly ones that are hung right side up and suspended from the bows.

The Algonquin were not known to treat the bark with any sort of preservative, though some smeared bear grease on the canoe's hull for a canoe race.

There has undoubtedly always existed a trade in birch bark in eastern Ontario and western Québec. In prehistoric times, birch bark for canoes likely was traded among builders. And when fur trade canoes were made at various posts, such as at Grand Lake Victoria, the Hudson's Bay Company probably traded in rolls of birch bark. There is a photo by Charles Macnamara of a Hudson's Bay Company fur trade canoe from Grand Lake Victoria coming into Kipawa, Québec, with rolls of birch bark for trade. And according to Lina Nottaway of Barrière Lake, the Barrière Indians used to take rolls of birch bark to Waswanipi because the Indians there had no big rolls of birch bark.

A large birch with good bark meant a lot to the Algonquin. They could make a canoe from its outer bark, tea from the inner bark, and paddles and snowshoe frames from the wood.

Cedar

Most wooden members of the canoe were made of cedar. This ordinarily includes the ribs, sheathing, and stem-piece, but not the thwarts. The stem-piece occasionally was made of ash, taken from the base of the tree so no bending would be required.

Gunwales were usually made of cedar, but occasionally of spruce, pine, and in one known case, ash.

The builder looks for cedar that is knotfree. In the case of gunwales, this means a clear section 5 m (16 ft.) along the trunk. Some builders take cedar from just one side of the trunk if the other side has visible knots or branches; others look for a trunk that is clear all the way around.

After the builder locates a suitable tree, he cuts it down and cuts a log 5 m (16 ft.) long. If he is using a chain saw, he may make a cut about 2 cm (1 in.) deep in the top end of the log to begin a split. This cut helps greatly to start the split, which will be executed with hand tools. Splits are made from the top end toward the butt end, unless an uneven piece has to be split off.

The split also can be started with a wedge. Algonquin builders in recent years have used a hardwood or steel wedge or a common ax. Hardwood wedges can be hewn from a felled tree by making a roughly transverse cut in the log, followed by a diagonal cut. For the next wedge, another roughly transverse cut is made at the head of the diagonal cut farther along the log. These cuts should be roughly transverse, so that the axis of the head lines up at exact right angles with the body of the wedge.

To split the cedar, the wedge is driven into the top of the log with a wooden mallet or ax. The split travels down the log as the builder drives the wedge in deeper. As soon as the split opens somewhat, another wedge is put in the top of the log in the widening split. As this is driven in, the split widens further. If the split is not clean and strips of wood hold the two halves together, those strips are chopped out with an ax.

Once the log is split in half, one half is

placed bark side up on a support (another log or clump of earth) that holds the top end up sufficiently so that the builder can get clear swings at it with his mallet or ax. This half is split in half again at right angles to the surface of the bark.

If the quarter log is still quite thick, it may be halved yet again in the same direction. If it is a little more manageable and small enough to be levered with the knee, it can be split in the same direction as the annual rings.

In a more limber piece of gunwale stock, and in rib stocks and sheathing stock, if a split starts going off to one side, it is levered in the other direction. The builder has his helper place a knee a few centimeters in front (toward the butt end) of the split, and he carefully attempts to bring the split back to center. If he is working alone, he may use the fork of a tree to achieve this same leverage.

If there is substantially more wood remaining at the butt end than at the top end, the builder can split off the excess to make his job of carrying out the wood that much easier.

The batten from which the gunwale is split is often soaked in water before the finest splitting is done. This seems to help in splitting the cedar. Nevertheless, wet cedar sometimes has a tendency to fray, so some builders, like Basil Dewachie of Maniwaki, put the cedar in the sun to dry it a bit before working it with a crooked knife.

It is preferable to split the gunwales from a batten of even dimensions. To make it even, the builder takes a batten and puts one end on his shoulder and the other end on the ground. Then he works up and down the batten with an ax until it has even dimensions. He may also finish the batten with the crooked knife to make it quite even. When it is twice the thickness of the gunwale he desires, the builder splits it.

The builder here exercises great care because of the value of the wood by this time. He starts the split at the top end of the batten and works it slowly down to the butt end. As with most other splitting, if the split starts to go to one side, he levers it the other way just beyond the split.

After this gunwale batten is split, only minor touches may be necessary with the crooked knife to get it to inwale or outwale dimensions.

For ease in working and to lessen the chance of breakage, the gunwales and caps usually are immersed in the lake until it is time to use them.

Rib stock is cut and split in the same way as gunwale stock. Ribs are shorter, and therefore suitable straight cedar is not as hard to locate. Rib stock as taken from the woods is usually 1.5 m (4½ ft.) long or shorter. It can be half a log, or it can be nearly finished ribs, depending upon how much time the builder spends taking down the stock in the woods before transporting it. (Finished ribs are commonly 5 cm [2 in.] wide by 1 cm [³/₈ in.] thick.) Because the stock is shorter, and because there is more of it and it is less valuable, the splitting of the ribs proceeds at a much faster rate than splitting of gunwales or sheathing.

In locating gunwale stock, the builder must exercise care. To set up the inwale assembly properly, the inwales should be straight and not curved. This is not so critical with rib stock, however, as ribs have to be steamed and bent to go into the canoe. Most builders feel that if ribs come from a slightly bent trunk, it will not make a great deal of difference. Jim Jerome was an exception to this way of thinking. He walked far in the woods to locate rib stock that was as straight as possible, even though clear, slightly curved stock could be had very easily.

The rib stock is cut in the woods to the length of the finished rib in the canoe plus 10 cm (4 in.) more on each end, so that the ends will come above the gunwales when the ribs are first bent to allow for them to be cut precisely later. Cutting the rib stock too short at this time would result in the finished ribs being too short, while leaving the stock too long would create more work for the builder, from carrying out more wood to working many extra inches on each rib with the crooked knife.

When working the ribs with a crooked knife, most of the Algonquin builders sat on a stump, while supporting the near end of the rib across the knees. The crooked knife was worked toward the carver. Some of these knives, like those used by Isaac Nottaway of Barrière Lake and his father Louis, were made from the rib bone of a moose. The blade was 10 cm (4 in.) to 12.5 cm (5 in.) long; the handle was crooked cedar or tanned hide wrapped around the end of the bone. In later years, the Barrière builders used steel blades made from bucksaws or files or bought from the Hudson's Bay Company.

The builder usually made extra ribs, as some might break in bending. If there were forty-four ribs in the finished canoe, he might make fifty-four. Jocko Carle once broke twenty-two ribs for a canoe, probably because he used thicker ribs than did most other builders.

Sheathing battens are fashioned with care, as sheathing is difficult to split. These battens are like perfectly shaped boards of dimensional lumber. The builder hand-splits a log and carves the batten to evenness with a crooked knife. As the batten is split thinner and thinner, the splitting becomes more and more precise. A knife is used to start the split, and then the fingers are used to continue the split. The pieces of sheathing must be supported with the hands very carefully across their full width while they are being split, or they will break.

After the sheathing battens are carefully split and trimmed up, they are soaked in water for several days while other work on the canoe progresses, as dry battens are more likely to split unevenly.

Sheathing battens may be 1.5 m (5 ft.) or longer. The finished pieces of sheathing may be from 8 to 10 cm (3 to 4 in.) wide and are usually quite thin, often as thing as 2 mm ($^2/_{25}$ in.). They must be fashioned very evenly.

The headboard or manboard is straight in Maniwaki but is often bellied outboard in Barrière Lake. In both areas, however, the headboard is often omitted. The Abnaki canoe has a thin headboard that is bellied toward the bow. Most Algonquin, in adopting the Abnaki form, nevertheless retained features of their old-style canoe. The Algonquin *wâbanäki tcîmân* often had a thicker, vertical headboard that was bracketed by a longitudinal strut to the stem-piece, though this is not often seen today. The headboard and stem-piece were joined outside the canoe and placed together into the bow.

Spruce Root

Lashing for the gunwales and bows of a canoe is done with spruce root. Most of the builders in western Québec used white spruce, though jackpine or even basswood bark may be used. According to Lina Nottaway, white spruce and jackpine root are stronger than black spruce or tamarack.

The Barrière builders occasionally decorated their canoes by dyeing the spruce root used to lash the gunwales. They would use raspberries, strawberries, or chokecherries for red dye, and blueberries for blue. Berries of one color were boiled, then the spruce root was added. The blue and red root lashings thus produced were then used at alternate spots on the gunwale.

Spruce root is more easily obtained in open areas, where the roots are not crossed with those of other trees, as they are likely to be in the woods. A pasture in current use should be avoided, as the ground will be packed hard and the roots will be difficult to dig up. Jocko Carle and William Commanda found their white spruce on wooded former farms.

To harvest the roots, the builder goes a meter or a little more from the base of the tree, and starts digging or scraping at the ground with the back of an ax head or other tool until a root is located. Lina Nottaway points out that it is easier to harvest roots in the spring, because the ground is moist and roots are closer to the surface.

When a root is located, it is cut and pulled out of the ground away from the tree. Often it will be intertwined with another root and may have to be fed under it. In pulling the root from the ground, care must be taken to avoid pulling the little side roots out of the main root in the direction of the tree. If this is done, the side roots can take with them a section of the main root, making the finished root that goes into the canoe unsightly.

Roots are pulled out for their entire length and can sometimes be as long as 7 m (22 ft.). When sufficient roots are pulled from the ground for a canoe, the builder rolls them into a coil. This coil may be as much as 70 cm (2 ft.) in diameter and 10 kg (20 lbs.) in weight.

Returning to camp, the builder may soak the roots in water for a few days while he is working on other parts of the canoe, or he (or his wife) may start preparation of the root right away if it looks fresh and if he is freed up from his other labors on the canoe.

Before starting to split the root, the builder may elect to take the bark off. This he does by pulling the root through a slit in a stick that has been fixed in the ground. The slit is just large enough to allow the root to be pulled through. This is a particularly laborious task. If any of the bark is difficult to remove, the root is put in boiling water for a few minutes until the bark is loosened.

To split the root, the builder always starts from the thick tree end. The little side roots on the main root usually tend to come out on opposite sides on the same plane. If this is the case, the split is made on the same plane as these side roots. The goal is to ensure that the finished root, when lashed in the canoe, will be clean and free of specks where any side branches may have grown. The side roots can be removed before or after splitting.

Most builders in western Québec held the root split between the fingers of both hands and guided the split with their fingers. Others held the end of one half in the mouth and the end of the other half in one hand, guiding the split with the other hand. As with cedar, if the split started to go to one side, it would be levered.

After the root is split in half, any remaining side roots are cut off at the base with a sharp

knife. Often the root is then quartered and the center part split out.

Once the roots have been prepared, they are again coiled until the builder is ready to use them.

In some canoes, the root is very evenly prepared and lashed, and gets narrower from center thwart to bows. In such cases, it is likely that the builder separated the just-prepared root by width so that it could later be lashed in such a methodical way.

In notes recorded in the early 1930s, Adney describes spruce root preparation by the Algonquin:

The roots when prepared for birch bark sewing are seldom more than a quarter of an inch in width and in the finer wrought portions of the same canoe may not be more than an eighth of an inch in diameter. It is desirable that these lie as flat as possible, so the root stripped of covering of bark will be split in several ways. A smallish root may be halved, and then shaved to more flatness if necessary. Algonkins of the Ottawa will take a root of three-eighths inch and split off a "slab" each side of a flat core. Another way is to quarter, and shave flat. Dried out roots are softened preferably in hot water at the moment of using. All splitting is done by Indians in the same fashion: started with the knife, then one side taken in the teeth, the other in one hand, the fingers of the other hand guiding and controlling the split as the ends are pulled apart. Now as there is but little strain on the stitching at the ends and a very powerful strain along the middle section from rib tension, it must be that the overwhipping withstands better a pulling strain than the other stitch. We can only explain its use the full length of the canoe in the Algonkin-Ojibway area by the fact that the women who make the birch baskets and who also sewed the canoes chanced to fall into using the same stitch for both thinking of its tightness rather than its resistance to pull.

Builder Patrick Maranda would collect in May all the root he would need for several canoes to be made during the summer and would split it at once, leaving the bark on. Then he would roll it in coils and leave it in the shade of a tree. When he was ready to make a canoe, he would take as much root as necessary, soak it, and then boil it before using it.

Other Materials

The thwarts are made of yellow birch, white birch, or ash. Ash is preferred for its qualities of flexibility. The wood is usually used green. The thwart batten is split out of the log in much the same way as a rib. As a general rule, the builder gets off as much wood as he can first by splitting, then by taking the piece down with the ax, and finally by finishing with a crooked knife. This allows as much wood as possible to be taken off less laboriously than with the crooked knife.

In the *wâbanäki tcîmân*, virtually the only model made in Golden Lake and western Québec in recent decades, the stem-piece is usually made of cedar. The stem-piece batten (often 4 cm [1¹/₂ in.] by 1.5 cm [⁵/₈ in.]) is split at right angles from the surface of the tree—in the opposite direction as the ribs. A

Mrs. David Manatch splitting spruce root for canoe at Lac Barrière, 1929. (Photo courtesy Museum of the American Indian, Heye Foundation.)

cord of basswood or other material is tied one-third of the way from one end of the stem-piece. The cedar is split in laminations down to that point, leaving the other two-thirds unsplit. The one-third that is to be split is split first in half down to the basswood binding, which stops it. Then one of the halves is split again, but this time unequally, in what might be called off-center splitting, as there is more wood on one side than on the other. It is a rather difficult thing to do, and often the canoe builder uses a knife to score ahead of the split or to guide it. In the finished bow, the split part will form the curve of the lower stem-piece, while the unsplit portion will mount toward the peak and usually has a tumblehome.

After the laminations are split, the stem-piece is soaked in water, sometimes for a day or two. Then boiling water is poured over it, and it is bent to the desired bow profile. Once this curvature has been achieved, it can be tied to form, or it can be placed against a flat board and nails hammered into the board alongside the stem-piece so that it holds its form while drying. A second stem-piece can be put on top of the first to be held to form by the nails. The stem-pieces are left to dry for a few days while other work proceeds on the canoe.

To gum the canoe, the canoe maker gathers resin from white spruce, black spruce, or pine trees, but not balsam. The builder puts the resin in a container over a fire to melt. Once it has melted, he puts it in a piece of fabric that has sticks at both ends. The sticks are turned in opposite directions, and the gum is extruded, the impurities remaining in the fabric.

The builder then puts the gum in water and boils it. The good gum rises to the top and is skimmed off, while the bad gum goes to the bottom.

Spruce gum is then mixed with bear grease, lard, grease from fish, or moose fat to temper it. It must not be too greasy, or it will run easily in the sun, but must have enough grease to prevent it from cracking too easily. One way of testing this is to put a strip of birch bark in the melted mixture and then submerge the strip in cold water. After the mixture hardens on the bark strip, it is bent back and forth. If it cracks easily, more grease is added. If it does not crack but is quite greasy, that may mean that there is too much grease, so more gum is

added to the mixture. If it does not crack and the hardened gum is not too greasy to the touch, the mixture is acceptable. Jocko Carle used another method to test the mixture. He raised the stirring stick from the melted mixture: If the resulting filament of material cracked, then he added more gum.

The gum mixture is quite important. If there is not sufficient grease, the gum mixture on the bow or gores can crack if the canoe strikes a rock or even when it comes to shore or a dock. The gum mixture is also more fragile in cold weather. If there is too much grease, the gum can run from the gores in the hot sun or if the canoe is stored in a warm place where the air does not move around. Some canoe builders mixed their gum keeping in mind the time of year when the canoe would be most used.

A protective piece of basswood or cedar bark or a canvas strip is placed over the chin of the bow before gumming. This gives more body to the gumming, and the gum mixture is less likely to chip and fall off.

Commercially produced pine rosin has sometimes been used instead of spruce gum in recent years by builders in western Québec. It is mixed with grease in the manner described above, as it appears to have pretty much the same properties as spruce gum. Roofing tar has also been used frequently; in this case no grease is necessary.

Other tempering agents, in addition to bear grease, have been tried: commercial lard and grease from fish. At least one builder, Patrick Maranda of Barrière Lake, used the fat from walleye to temper gum.

Wooden pegs have been used in canoes, especially in the gunwale. Pegs that go horizontally between inwale and outwale must be hardwood. Most builders favor ironwood or maple for these pegs. Softer woods, like white spruce, may be used for vertical pegs: in the inwale and outwale, to hold the gunwale cap down. The ribs in a canoe exert enormous pressure upward, and these horizontal pegs are, along with the inwales, the main members resisting this pressure. In older canoes, hardwood pegs sometimes have been bent at right angles by this pressure.

The pegs that go down through the gunwale cap into the gunwale usually are square and made of the same wood as the horizontal pegs in the gunwale. In the upward sweep of the gunwale near the bows, sometimes a peg does not hold the cap to the gunwale snugly and the cap comes up. To prevent this, some builders rub the pegs across sticky spruce gum before pounding them into the cap.

Canoe paddles are made of ash, white birch, yellow birch, maple, cedar, spruce, or black cherry. A skilled man with a crooked knife could make a paddle quite quickly. This was illustrated in a photo series in *Life* magazine in 1941. Basil Dewachie of Maniwaki once was traveling with a tourist, when the latter lost his paddle in a rapids. The two went ashore, and with ax and crooked knife, Dewache fashioned another good paddle in an hour.

CANOE ASSEMBLY

In recent decades, most Algonquin of western Québec and eastern Ontario made building beds on the ground. Exceptions to this were Dan Sarazin and William Commanda, who employed building beds of boards raised from the ground about 60 cm (2 ft.).

For the earthen bed, the ground is dug up and any roots or stones removed. A bit of nearby sand might be mixed into the dirt, but the bed itself is not made in beach sand, because it would not provide enough support to hold up the side stakes. The ground must be loose enough to receive the stakes yet solid enough to hold them, as the stakes may have to be put in and taken out several times during the building process.

In examples seen, the building bed was level, whether it was on the ground or a raised platform. In Golden Lake in the late 1920s, for example, Tommy Sarazin and Dan Sarazin made a level building bed with a 15-cm (8-in.)-wide board sunk along the middle to ensure a true line for the bottom.

If the builder has more than one roll of bark that he is considering for use in the canoe, he may at this point take them out, unroll them, and see which would be the best in terms of length and quality for the canoe he plans to build.

The bark will be weighted down with a building frame to form the bottom of the canoe. In recent years in Maniwaki, Jocko Carle and William Commanda used a building frame of two pieces of plywood, which they cut out by bending a gunwale to the proper curvature over a standard plywood sheet. The Barrière

David Makakons (right) and his son Nias unrolling bark on their building bed at Lac Barrière in 1929. (Photo courtesy Museum of the American Indian, Heye Foundation.)

David Makakons removing excess bark before beginning canoe construction at Lac Barrière. (Photo courtesy Museum of the American Indian, Heye Foundation.)

The Lac Barrière building bed and frame of David Makakons, 1929. (Photo courtesy Museum of the American Indian, Heye Foundation.)

Lake building frame was a single piece made by taking two long battens and separating them with many crosspieces at fairly regular intervals. The Maniwaki building frame had basically the same beam as the inwale assembly. In Barrière Lake, the frame was almost always narrower than the inwale assembly. The Algonquin would sometimes intentionally make the building frame narrower than normal to create a faster canoe.

Dan Sarazin's building frame for a 3.6-m (12-ft.) to 4.5-m (15-ft.) canoe in the late 1920s, according to Adney, was made of two strips of cedar 3.8 cm (1¹/₂ in.) by 1.9 cm (³/₄ in.) notched and tied together at the ends, the wood bent edgewise. The two strips were held apart by crosspieces of cedar 2.5 cm (1 in.) wide and 4.5 cm (1³/₄ in.) deep, set edgewise and notched at the ends 1.9 cm (³/₄ in.) (the depth of the two side strips). The tops of the crosspieces were round-beveled, with holes near the ends to enable the ends to be tied to the sides. The crossbar at the center was 50 cm (19¹/₂ in.) long measured inside the side strips, giving a beam overall for the building frame of 58.5 cm (23 in.) at the center thwart. This building frame was significantly narrower than the beam of the finished canoe, which may have been about 80 cm (31 in.) to 85 cm (33 in.) outside at the center thwart. The crossbars for the intermediate thwarts on either side of the center thwart were 40 cm (15³/₄ in.) long. The crossbars for the end thwarts were 15.25 cm (6 in.) long and were located about 30 cm (12 in.) from the end of the building frame. The tying was done with basswood bark.

When Jocko Carle made canoes in the 1930s, he most often used the old Maniwaki-area Algonquin method for a building frame. That was to use the inwale assembly as a building frame, raising it later so that it came to proper inwale height.

The building bed is raked carefully so that it is as level as possible, the leveling being done by sight. The building frame is centered carefully on the bed, and the stakes are driven into the ground vertically where they will be after the bark is unrolled on the bed. Then the stakes are removed and laid away from their holes and the building frame taken from the bed.

Next, the bark is unrolled. Before the builder proceeds with the construction, he and his helper look over the bark carefully and may kneel next to it to pick blemishes from the white side, often using a knife, and to take one or more layers from the bark where it appears too thick. When this process is completed, the building frame is centered on the sheet, exactly over the area where it had been placed on the building bed before the bark was unrolled. The bark is then moved under the frame to center it properly. As good bark is a scarce commodity, the builder takes every care when he is centering it to get the most from all available bark, sometimes measuring how much bark extends beyond each bow.

For centering the bark from side to side, Jim Jerome uses a straightedge about 5 m (16 ft.) long, simply a gunwale-like batten of cedar that he carved. He places this straightedge on the centerline of the building frame, and it extends beyond each bow. He also uses the straightedge to score a dull line straight outboard from each bow. In bending the bark to form the bow, he is guided by this line, and the slight score helps the bark to bend on the correct line.

At the location of the future center thwart, the building frame is now moved from side to side until there is an equal amount of bark on each side of the frame. With luck, the builder has found a sheet of bark that is wide enough so that it will not have to be pieced on the sides to achieve the required beam. If pieces must be added to the sides, they are sewn onto this bark that extends out from each side of the building frame.

When the builder has the bark centered under the frame, he weights the frame down with about 200 kg (450 lbs.) of stones.

Then gores are cut in the bark sheet. The gores should be as straight as possible. They are cut at a bevel and are streamlined bow to stern or, in some canoes, bow to center thwart. Gores should be vertical in the finished canoe. But because the bark sheet (the hull) curves to follow the frame toward the bow, the gores toward the bow would slant if an adjustment were not made. Jim Jerome slants the last gore or two toward the bow as he cuts them in the bark sheet. When the sides of the bark sheet are put up, these gores will be vertical.

The gores are carefully cut to the building frame. Cutting the bark too quickly can result in the knife's going off in one direction or the other. Because the gores are cut to the building frame, the width of the building frame of a finished canoe can be determined by measuring the distance across the bottom of the hull to the lower ends of the gores on either side.

When the gores are cut, and sometimes before cutting them, the builder may make a dull score with a sharp stick along the outer edge of the building frame. This helps the bark bend up evenly when the bark sides are put up. Hot water is often ladled alongside the building frame for the same purpose.

As the bark sides are put up, the outer stakes are placed in the holes that were made earlier. Long fairing pieces may be put inboard and outboard at this point to help form the hull. Each outer stake is tied with a basswood or other cord (Patrick Maranda used the inner bark of the cedar) to its mate directly on the other side of the canoe across the gunwale.

Inner stakes are put inboard immediately across the gunwale from the outer stakes. These inner stakes are beveled on the bottom and pry against the edge of the building frame. They are lashed to their mates just across the gunwale in a temporary way so that they can be untied and tied again readily when the inwale assembly and outwales are put in place and when minor adjustments have to be made.

Dan Sarazin used fourteen cedar inner stakes. They were from 50 to 65 cm (20 to 25 in.) in length, 3.8 cm (1¹/₂ in.) wide, and 1.9 to 2.5 cm (³/₄ to 1 in.) thick, gradually tapering to a wedge point.

At this point, the inwale assembly must be fixed. The inwale assembly is made in a couple of different ways. Essentially it is formed of the inwales as they will finally go in the canoe. But the thwarts at this point may be permanent or temporary. The common Maniwaki practice was to have temporary thwarts until somewhat later in the process. In Maniwaki, these temporary thwarts have two holes in each end. The temporary crossbars hold the inwales apart, and a cord is tied through the holes and around the inwale to hold them in place.

In the 1920s, Dan Sarazin separated the inwales with the crossbars and nailed a small nail through the crossbar ends, resting on top of and into the inwale.

Jim Jerome used permanent thwarts of yellow birch at this point, though they were not lashed in place. Only the mortises and tenons were cut.

Jocko Carle has suggested that the inwale may be the most important structural member of the canoe. Though it is hand-split and hard-carved, it should be as straight as a board sawn at the mill. The inwale is 3.3 cm (1³/₄ in.) high by 2 cm (³/₄ in.) wide at the center thwart. These measurements are pretty much maintained until outboard of the end thwarts, where they are reduced somewhat to allow for bending for the upward sheer of the bow. The inwale is beveled at about a 45-degree angle where the rib ends will later go. This bevel is on the underside of the inwale and against the bark. The bevel is continuous and goes outboard beyond the end thwarts, as the ribs must. A builder once forgot to put the bevel in at this point. He discovered his omission much later, just prior to bending the ribs, and had to cut out bevels, very laboriously, between root lashings.

The center thwart is usually 5.5 cm (2¹/₈ in.) wide and 1.2 cm (¹/₂ in.) thick. In nearly all the canoes, the center thwart had a shoulder near the gunwale for tying the tumpline for the portage carry. The end of the thwart is mortised into the inwale only; it goes only as far as the bark.

David Makakons has turned up the sides to begin construction on this canoe. The flare suggests that the building frame is significantly narrower than the gunwale frame. (Photo courtesy Museum of the American Indian, Heye Foundation.)

Golden Lake in 1928. The outwales on this canoe have not yet been raised to their final sheer. The two supports are in place over the end thwarts, which will allow the canoe to be raised slightly off the bed for rib bending. (Photo courtesy Museum of the American Indian, Heye Foundation.)

In a typical Maniwaki assembly, temporary thwarts would take the place of permanent thwarts at this point. They would not be mortised into the inwale but would be tied snugly to the inwale by cord.

Jim Jerome would have completed all his thwarts and mortises by this point. The inwale assembly was therefore much like it would be in the finished canoe and really awaited only the pegging and lashing of the thwart ends. Jim also bent the inwale ends up before they went into the canoe so that right away they achieved the final sheer. How Jocko Carle achieved his sheer will be described later.

Measuring sticks were used to mark off locations for the ribs and lashings on the inwales and sometimes on the outwales. These intervals were often 5 cm (2 in.) wide, alternating lashing and ribs. The thwart ends came to the inwale at a lashing locus.

After the gores have been cut and the sides put up, the inwale assembly is then put in the canoe. This assembly is fixed at its proper height by using measuring sticks—sticks with shoulders on them cut at specific heights. The shoulders may be 15 cm (6 in.) high, more or less, depending on the desired finished depth of the canoe. Four measuring sticks normally are used. The bottoms of these sticks rest on the building frame.

In calculating the finished depth of the canoe in relation to these measuring sticks, the builder must add the height of the shoulders, the thickness of the building frame, and the total height of the inwale and gunwale cap. This gives him only an approximate depth of the finished canoe. The amount that the hull will belly out when the ribs are later forced in also must be factored in.

Jocko Carle measured with the sticks from the building frame to the bottom of the inwale. This measure was kept exactly the same all along the gunwale at all points between the two intermediate thwarts.

Jim Jerome took his measure from the building frame to the underside of the center and intermediate thwarts.

Dan Sarazin employed the shouldered measuring sticks. The foot of the stick sat on the top of the building frame, with the shoulders of the stick supporting the gunwale frame at the ends of the three longer crossbars. A single measuring stick was under the middle of the short end crossbar.

The height of the shoulders of the measuring sticks is graduated: 24 cm (9½ in.) at the middle crossbar, 26 cm (10¼ in.) at the second crossbars, and 29 cm (11½ in.) at the end one. In this way, the desired sheer is achieved.

The builder must constantly check these measures as he sets up the inwale frame to the outwales, for as he is adjusting one part of the gunwale, another measure may fall out from under the inwale or the thwart. A centimeter error at this point could conceivably result in a malformed canoe. Likewise, he must continually ensure, especially at this part of the building process, that the bows line up with each other properly.

The outwale may measure 3 cm (1⅙ in.) high by 1 cm (⅜ in.) wide. As the inwale is the main structural member of the canoe, the outwale does not have to be as thick; it only functions to help form the gunwale, with the bark sandwiched between the inwale and outwale.

If the inwale assembly has been used as the building frame, it is now raised from the bark sheet and fixed to the proper inwale height using the shouldered measuring sticks. The outwale is then set outboard of the bark and the inwale. When the outwale is even with the inwale, the two are clamped together carefully all along the gunwale with metal C-clamps or wooden clamps.

If the bark sheet is not wide enough at the center thwart, side pieces of bark are now sewn to the main sheet. The eyes in the side pieces go in the same direction as the eyes in the main sheet of bark. The pieces are fitted down inboard of the main sheet and down as far as possible between the building frame and the main sheet, the bark of the latter extending inches up along the side piece. They are stitched together with a harness-maker stitch, with both ends of a single strand passed in opposite directions through holes made with an awl. Then these strands are drawn tight in opposite directions, leaving a smooth exterior.

After the stitching, the surplus bark above the stitching is trimmed with a knife fairly close to the stitching, 2 cm (¾ in.) or less. The advantage of this technique is that the awl is less likely to split the bark than if used close to the edge. This was how the fur trade canoes were stitched.

The builder continually watches that all his measures remain correct and in place.

Reinforcing bark is sometimes added before the inwales and outwales receive their final clamping. The reinforcing bark is a piece or pieces that usually go from bow to bow. Their upper edge is even with the top surface of the gunwale, and they extend about 10 cm (4 in.) below the outwale. The reinforcing bark helps to keep water from splashing through the root holes beneath the gunwales, and also has a decorative effect (which can also be approximated by scraping a similar design in winter bark beneath the gunwales). These pieces of reinforcing bark have serrated, scalloped, or straight bottom edges.

The sheer lines are fixed differently at this point by different builders. The sheer in Jocko Carle's canoe outboard of the intermediate thwarts has not yet been established. He will wait to raise the inwale assembly, and the outwales to match it, until after he has lashed the gunwales to the intermediate thwarts or slightly beyond, though he may at this time prop each end of the inwale assembly up so that they get physically used to the upward sweep. Jim Jerome, on the other hand, has already raised the inwales to form his sheer, so the outwales may be raised and clamped as well; thus his sheer is established before the gunwale lashing begins.

When the side pieces are sewn to the main sheet, the builder again has to check his clamping of the gunwales. In the Maniwaki canoe, the walls now have to be vertical and tightly pulled into the gunwale sandwich, held in place by the clamps.

With the gunwales clamped securely, the bark is trimmed down to the upper surface. Sometimes tongues are cut in the bark above the gunwales. These tongues are cut at every lashing locus or sometimes at every rib locus. These tongues are just long enough to fold down over the top surface of the inwale. They end at the inboard side of the inwale. Their purpose is to help resist the very strong upward pressure of the ribs later when the ribs are put into the canoe for their final insertion.

There are a number of ways in which the builder tries to guard against this pressure. The ribs are put into the canoe almost as tightly as the builder is able. Care must be taken to lash the gunwales properly and to do a good job pegging the inwale and outwale horizontally with good hardwood pegs. All these things, well done, help resist the eventual upward pressure of the ribs.

Hardwood dowels, often of ironwood, are used to peg the gunwale horizontally. The pegs are put through holes drilled at every lashing locus, so that the pegs will be hidden by the lashing later. Adney believed that the old way of preparing the gunwales was to have them lashed entirely with roots, pegs being used only at sufficient intervals to hold the gunwales in position until the bark could be trimmed and the sewing done.

But when nails began to be taken note of, builders were not sure whether nails would hold. According to Adney, "In every little thing the native American craftsman was conscious of a reason. He was slow to adopt nails in the canoe and then to the last in many cases only in the long stretches of the gunwale, not for fastening the crossbars, not at the ends where the wood being slender the root wrapping was sounder construction." A canoe built at Oka, Québec, by Algonquin Peter White Duck thus showed a nail and wrapping alternately.

In 1927 Adney saw a large model from the "Têtes de Boule" (probably Algonquin bands) who were by now accustomed to nails with gunwales fully group wrapped, with a peg in addition between each wrapping. The model had the gunwale cap nailed, whereas, according to Adney, it should have been pegged. He thought that perhaps in localities where nailing had been the rule for a considerable period of time, canoe makers who set out to build for a customer did not feel secure that roots were sufficient to hold, just as formerly they feared the nails would not hold. Adney said that not until clinchable wire nails came into general use, about 1868 in central Canada, was there any appreciable use of nails where roots had been previously used.

Dan Sarazin would now chisel out the mortises for the permanent thwarts, which were then set in place. Sometimes he felt it desirable to spread the gunwales a little, making the canoe 2 or 3 cm ($^3/_4$ or $1^1/_4$ in.) wider, giving more sheer to the gunwales and at the same time lifting the ends if the canoe was to have a rocker bottom. Adney said that great care had to be taken in doing so.

Now the gunwale lashing begins. The gunwale is lashed at the places on the gunwale earlier marked out. There 5-cm (2-in.) spots for lashing alternate with 5-cm (2-in.) spots where the rib ends come up under the inwale.

For making holes in the bark, an awl with a triangular blade is preferred over one with a cylindrical blade. When the latter is put through the bark, the bark often splits above and below the hole. With a triangular-bladed awl, first the blade is pushed through the bark, and then a round hole is made by twisting the blade.

For each lashing, five or six holes are made below the gunwale. The root end is first anchored, perhaps between the inwale and the outwale, perhaps under the gunwale. The root is then passed over the gunwale and two or three times through each hole. When the 5-cm (2-in.) section has been lashed, either the root end is anchored once again or the root is passed outboard under the gunwale to the next lashing locus and the lashing is continued. Patrick Maranda used one piece of root for each locus, rather than continuous lashing. He finished this locus with a knot that was inboard and hidden under the root.

Neither Jim Jerome nor Jocko Carle would lash the thwarts when they came to them along the gunwale during the lashing process. Both would wait to lash the thwarts until the gunwales were almost entirely lashed and the building frame removed from the bottom of the canoe. As Jocko Carle lashed the first lashing outboard of the intermediate thwarts (these are four different places on the gunwales), he would raise the bow of the assembly up on each end. Then he would lash two more spots, then raise the bow of the inwale assembly again, and so on. Thus he achieved the sheer in his canoes.

When the lashing is completed outboard of the end thwarts along the gunwales, the thwarts are lashed in. Often a hardwood peg is put down through the inwale and the thwart end at the mortise. When a thwart is pegged in, it is then lashed in. The spruce root passes through the same number of holes under the lashing locus on the gunwale, but this time,

instead of simply circling the gunwale, it goes through two or three holes made in the thwart not far out from the inwale.

Jocko Carle would take his building frame, in two plywood halves, out of the canoe just before the center thwart was lashed. Jim Jerome's one-piece building frame was taken out before lashing the intermediate thwart and the end thwart on one side.

After the lashing is completed along the gunwales, the builder puts the stem-piece into the bows. He tries to see that the bottom of the stem-piece sits flat against the bark and that the top of the stem is angled back inboard with the right tumblehome. In the canoes of Jocko Carle, and one or two other members of the Carle family of Maniwaki, there was no tumblehome and the stem was vertical. This, however, was rather untypical of the bow profiles of the builders in eastern Ontario and western Québec.

As the stem-piece is pushed down so that it sits snug against the bark, the outwales may be pulled up as high as possible one last time. Then a peg is put through at the peak just under the ends of the outwales so that they can rest on it.

The canoe is then turned upside down on a table or something of the sort. The bark is trimmed to the profile of the stem-piece. Sometimes it is trimmed so that the bark sheets come together outboard of the stem-piece, and sometimes so that the ends of the sheet are flush with the edge of the stem-piece and the stem-piece is therefore visible.

When the bark is thus cut, an awl or drill is used to make holes through the center of the stem-piece and through the bark for the bow lashing. They are 2 to 3 cm (^{3}/4 to 1^1/4 in.) apart and are drilled from near the peak along the stem to just beyond where the cut finishes at the heel of the stem. The lashing of the bow is done with one long, solid piece of spruce root. Beginning on the heel of the stem-piece, the root is lashed in a double in-and-out stitch around the curve of the bow. From there, it is lashed in a double cross-stitch to a point just below the ends of the gunwales.

The ribs are all bent in one day, from center thwart to bow. Before the ribs are bent, the bottom of the canoe is swept and temporary sheathing is put in place to support the bark while the ribs are bent and while they are drying.

Careful builders put the widest, thickest ribs near the center thwart and narrow ribs toward the bows. Ribs are bent two at a time so that they can support each other. The pair is first laid across the gunwales, an equal amount extending outboard on either side. Then three or four finger lengths are measured from the inboard edge of the inwale, and that spot is marked off on the top rib of the pair. Some builders use a pencil, but a pencil mark, even if lightly drawn, will score the surface. This will not cause the rib to break, but there will be a crease in the wood at that point. Dan Sarazin used charcoal instead. The resulting mark was so lightly applied that the chances of scoring were greatly reduced.

After the ribs are marked, the rib pair is put into a container of water that is boiling over a fire. Then, holding one end of the rib pair in the boiling water with one hand, the builder ladles the water over the entire length of the ribs. Then the other end of the pair is put in the water and the ladling resumes. This whole process takes only two or three minutes.

Now the rib pair is bent. The bend is not made across the center part of the rib, but rather only at the two marked spots. The builder begins with the end that received the boiling water first, as it is now starting to cool. Care has to be taken to bend the rib pair a little at a time, or it might break. The knee is flexed against the rib pair every 2 cm (^{3}/4 in.) or so until it starts bending evenly. This is done then at the other mark.

The ends of the rib pair are then pressed toward each other in front of the builder so that he can judge for the proper curvature, a wide, flat-bottomed U shape, the bottom part to go against the bottom of the canoe.

The canoe builder then walks back to the canoe to put the first rib pair into the canoe next to the center thwart. He steps into the canoe and, with his helper, tries to fit the rib pair snugly against the bottom of the canoe and up against the sides. Then he takes the top rib and moves it to the rib location next outboard. Some builders, when advancing this top rib, turn it end for end to equalize the pressure from the bottom rib to the top.

The next rib pair to be bent is the one on the other side of the center thwart. Rib pairs are then bent all the way to the bows, first on one side of the center thwart, then on the other.

A binder is then put in the canoe. The binder is composed of two long battens put in the bottom of the canoe. Cross-pieces are wedged against the battens, causing them to exert strong outward pressure against the ribs. Short struts are placed vertically below the thwarts to the long battens. These force the binder down against the bottom as much as possible.

A binder in a canoe under construction, Maniwaki, 1929. There are four cross-pieces nailed across the gunwales to keep them from spreading under rib pressure. (Photo courtesy Museum of the American Indian, Heye Foundation.)

A canoe under construction at Maniwaki, 1929. The binder is in place, struts are forcing the sides apart, and another strut under the intermediate thwart is forcing the binder down. The gores are sewn— an unusual touch for a Maniwaki builder. (Photo courtesy Museum of the American Indian, Heye Foundation.)

David Makakons has inserted the ribs and is stretching the bark before the final placement of the sheathing— an unusual procedure. (Photo courtesy Museum of the American Indian, Heye Foundation.)

Fitting ribs in a canoe at the Hudson's Bay Company's Lac Barrière post, 1929. (Photo courtesy Museum of the American Indian, Heye Foundation.)

The builder examines the ribs to see that all of them are still bent properly. This is probably the last stage at which these adjustments can be made fairly easily.

It is very important after all this is done to fix across the gunwales battens that restrain the

A gunwale in cross section.

A gunwale assembly, looking inboard.

A rib with a beveled end.

Bow views of a River Désert wābanāki tcīmān.

outward pressure of the binder. If this is not done, the binder may burst the canoe, pulling out the thwarts from the gunwales. Six or eight crosspieces are either nailed or notched and fixed across the top of the gunwales.

When this is done, the canoe is left in the sun for a day or so to dry the ribs. While the ribs are drying, the canoe builder may attend to other matters, such as finishing the preparation of gum or making sure all the sheathing is ready for final placement in the canoe.

When the ribs are ready for final placement, the building bed is smoothed over once again. The canoe is placed right side up on the bed, the binder is removed, and the inside of the canoe is swept.

The thin pieces of cedar sheathing are removed from the lake where they have been soaking for a few days. They are laid out on a table for selection prior to placement in the canoe.

Although the ribs were bent and inserted to dry in the canoe from the center thwart to the bow, they are now wedged under the inwale starting from the bow and working toward the center thwart.

Pieces of sheathing line the inner hull between the ribs and the bark. The thin pieces cover the bark so that its white side (the outside of the tree and inner hull of the canoe) is not visible from the inboard side of the canoe, except where the sheathing does not quite reach the inner gunwale. The first piece of sheathing is placed next to the heel of the stempiece; this, of necessity, should be especially thin and flexible, as it has to follow the fold in the bark. This piece may be fitted under what is called a "frog," a piece of bark or wood positioned between the stem-piece end and the main bark sheet. Because of the pressure the stem-piece exerts against the bark at this point, sometimes the heel of the stem-piece may pierce the bark, so the added protection is a safeguard.

After the first piece of sheathing is laid on the bottom, other pieces are fitted overlapping, and against the stem-piece in the bow, up to the gunwales. The upper piece always overlaps the lower one so that sand and water are kept out from under the sheathing as much as possible. Some tribes fitted the sheathing edge-to-edge, but the Algonquin do not appear to have

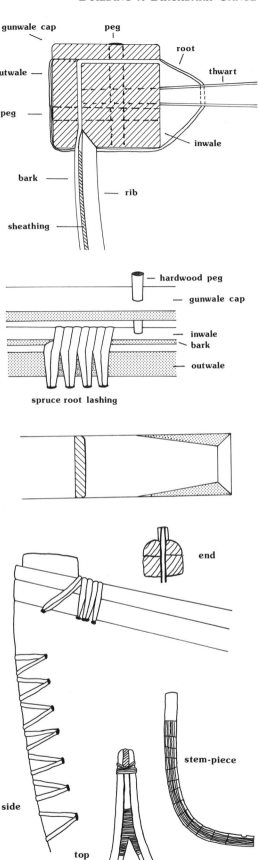

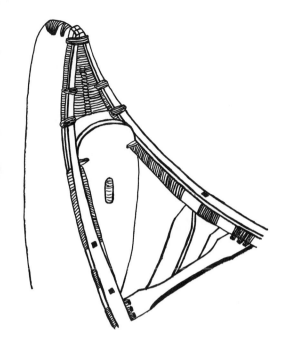

porarily. Alternatively, a dummy rib quickly made of sapwood may perform this function. More than one builder has, at this point, been heard to bemoan the fact that he did not have six arms.

In notes on the laying of the sheathing, Adney wrote in November 1932:

The manner of laying the sheathing is everywhere in the Eastern Woodlands area that of edge-to-edge carefully fitted, excepting in the inner area, the middle St. Lawrence to Lake Superior. . . . The St. Francis, Têtes de Boule, Algonkins and Ojibway as far as Lake Superior have the sheathings in often short lengths and overlapping not only use of short lengths such as four or five in the length of the canoe is certainly due to the scarcity of splitting cedar brought about by the removal of cedar by the lumbermen, and it is probable the side overlapping is also recent for although with patience and skill cedar may be split very thin, yet these sheaths are not merely split thin but are thinned at their edges only implying whittling that the superior steel knives can readily do but which the old stone or sling knife was by no means so well fitted for do-

done this. These sheathing pieces do not stay in place of their own accord (they are later held in place by the ribs), so one of the ribs is trimmed to hold the sheathing in place tem-

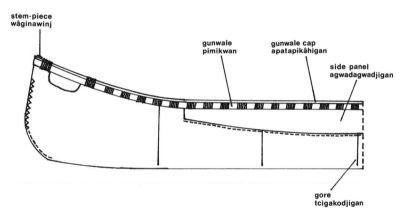

*The profile of an Algonquin
wâbanāki tcîmân, with the
parts labeled in English and
Algonquin.*

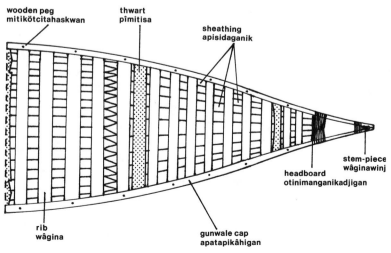

*A view of an Algonquin
wâbanāki tcîmân from above,
with the parts labeled in
English and Algonquin.*

An old-style Maniwaki canoe by Charlie Commanda, now at Lac Désert, Québec. The end piece of the sheathing does not extend under the heel of the stem-piece; the gores overlap bow to center thwart. (Photo by David Gidmark.)

(Right) An example of an Algonquin canoe with a sharp sheer at the bow. The end of the bark sheet is nailed to the stem-piece, which serves as the cutwater. (Photo by David Gidmark.)

(Below) An Algonquin wâbanǎki tcǐmân found at Lake Pemichigan, Gatineau Valley. Visible are two deck pieces, one of wood, the other of bark. (Photo by David Gidmark.)

ing. In an earlier period, we believe the sheathing was all laid edge-to-edge, and in the European period, the late 1600s when we have our first particulars of construction, the sheathing in the large canoes at least is described as being of twice the thickness of the birch bark, the varanges or ribs being three times the thickness of the bark.

In order for a rib to be cut off to the desired length, it is put in its planned location and pushed to the bottom of the canoe. A pencil line is drawn on the outboard side of the rib level with the top of the gunwale. The builder removes the rib, sits or kneels, and makes a bevel with his crooked knife at that point and on each side of the tip. The bevels face inboard.

The rib is taken back to the canoe, and the beveled ends are inserted under the inwale at a point between the two spruce root lashings, the bevel of the tip fitting with the bevel on the outboard side of the inwale next to the bark. Because the cedar is soft and can mark easily, a wooden driving stick is placed against the rib and is struck with a hammer to drive the rib in. Considerable pressure is exerted by the rib being forced into position. It is this pressure by the ribs in concert, along with the

general strength of the materials, that makes the hull of the birchbark canoe so strong and solid.

Birch bark takes time to adjust to the pressure of the ribs, so they are not pounded completely home to the vertical but are forced in short of the vertical. Hours later, they are pounded in the rest of the way. Some builders, such as Jim Jerome and Dan Sarazin, put a pair of posts at each end thwart and tie a cord from the posts to the end thwarts to raise the canoe slightly, leaving the bark to belly out a little and barely touch the ground. This allows for more convenient fitting of the ribs, as the weight of the canoe itself does not, in this manner, exert a resisting force onto the ribs. Another important reason for supporting the canoe slightly higher is so that the builder can observe the bottom of the canoe as he fits the ribs by pressure.

Spruce root lashings run the length of the gunwales, unless nails were used, as was often the case in recent decades. This lashing can be damaged by paddle strokes, so a gunwale cap—a long piece of cedar resembling one of the gunwales—is fashioned for each gunwale.

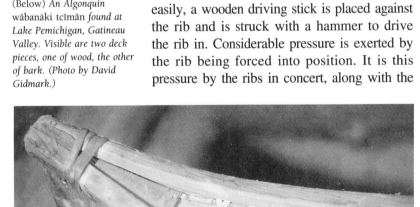

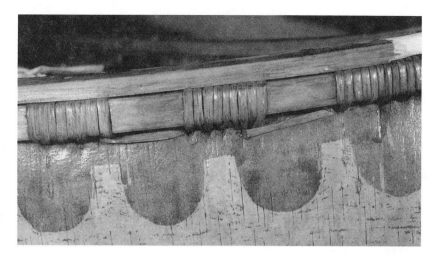

An Algonquin wâbanäki tcîmân of undetermined origin. The root thong is continued under the gunwale. The scallop design in the winter bark is a rather unusual one. (Photo by David Gidmark.)

It is longer than a gunwale at first (later shortened to finish properly at the bows) and slightly narrower than the gunwale-bark sandwich when seen in plan view.

The builder first centers this cap lengthwise at the center thwart. This is a two-person operation: One worker (often the builder's wife) holds the cap on top of the gunwale with both hands. A hole is drilled on either side of the center thwart through the cap and the inwale. A long, round (square with some builders) peg is inserted in each hole, and the gunwale cap is bent to conform to the curve of the gunwale by bending it slightly after each peg is added. In 1929, Adney examined an old-style Algonquin canoe at the Papineau estate at Montebello on the Ottawa River. To hold the gunwale caps to the gunwales, it had square cedar pegs. It is not unknown for the gunwale cap to break during this operation; the tapering in diameter of the peg, if it is pounded down too far, can split the cedar. The end of the gunwale cap narrows substantially toward the bow, so it would be difficult to put a peg through it without splitting it. Spruce root is therefore lashed around the gunwale and the gunwale cap at the same site in order to hold the latter in place.

Just beyond the stem-piece, the gunwales and caps are shaved off. These pinch the stem-piece as they are lashed together immediately inboard of it, though it has been the Golden Lake practice in recent years to lash the gunwale caps outboard of the stem-piece.

The small deck is made from a thick piece of birch bark or wood. Jocko Carle used birch bark, while David Makakons of Barrière Lake nearly always used birch wood. Jim Jerome

used bark and extended his deck-pieces below the outwales. The form of the deck-piece is one of a number of indicators that distinguish the birchbark canoes of various builders.

Some Algonquin builders made designs on their canoes. The dark rind of the winter bark

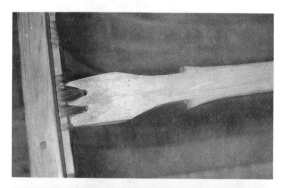

The lashing of the center thwart on what is probably a Rapid Lake canoe, possibly by Patrick Maranda. (Photo by David Gidmark.)

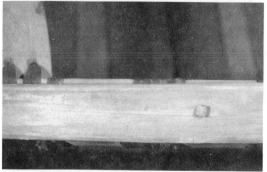

A square hardwood peg in the gunwale cap of the probable Rapid Lake canoe—this is the proper way of fixing a gunwale cap, with the cap centered and slightly narrower than the gunwale. (Photo by David Gidmark.)

The bellied headboard of the probable Rapid Lake canoe. The spruce root lashings over the gunwale cap are unusual. (Photo by David Gidmark.)

A Rapid Lake canoe constructed in the early 1960s, now at Désert Lake, Québec. This canoe is made of a single sheet of bark. (Photo by David Gidmark.)

The view from inboard the Rapid Lake canoe. The headboard is straight; the last rib is "broken." (Photo by David Gidmark.)

is first wet with a rag for a few minutes. The designs are traced with an awl point around fish, bear, or moose silhouettes. The rind is then scraped away from around the figure, leaving only the dark animal form on the bark.

Adney was told by Tommy Sarazin of Golden Lake that the decorations on the canoes were of "the animals the Indians hunted." On the same 1927 visit, Adney saw a canoe (built by Matt Bernard) decorated with fish and five-pointed stars.

In the late 1920s, a chief from Oka, Québec, recalled having seen, a few decades earlier, a brigade of about twelve large canoes come down the Ottawa. One of these canoes was decorated. On the bow it had an Indian's head with a feather, and on the stern, an arrow. Along the sides, on reinforcing bark as wide

as one's hand, were various animals—otters, minks, bears, moose—either painted in dull red paint or done in winter bark.

At Barrière Lake the designs scraped on winter bark included trees, flowers, and an Indian calling moose.

In the next step, gum is applied to the canoe. This is generally done by two persons. One holds the pan containing the hot gum, and the other uses a wooden spatula to apply the gum over the gores and the bows, covering all spots where water may pass through. On the bows, a strip of basswood bark or cloth is sometimes placed over the lower part of the root lashing to protect it, and the gum is applied over this protective strip. Alternatively, the gum may be applied directly to the lashing. When the gum has to be worked into place, the thumb is moistened with saliva so that the hot gum does not stick to the skin. Gum has to be attended to from time to time after it is applied to the canoe, particularly at the beginning of the season.

According to Lina Nottaway, a birchbark canoe can last twenty to forty years if taken care of. She says the canoe should never be left directly on the ground for a long period of time. It also is not good to let a birchbark canoe sit for a long time on leaves, as they will cause the bark to change color and start to rot. Her father, Isaac, kept his canoe on logs.

In an overnight camp, if there was more than one person, Nottaway would sleep with her head under the upturned canoe. If she was alone, she slept lengthwise under the canoe. She sometimes would go two or three weeks alone in a 4-m (13-ft.) canoe made by her father, Isaac.

According to Irene Jerome, Algonquin Indians would turn a birchbark canoe over at night for a temporary camp, but other than that they kept the canoe right side up overnight to lessen the chances of damage from bears. Anytime it rained, the canoe would be turned upside down to keep the ribs and sheathing from soaking up water and taking on a lot of weight.

For winter storage, a stand was made for the birchbark canoe under a tree. It was stored upside down.

To transport a birchbark canoe in winter time, it was carried on a handsleigh about 2.5 m (8 ft.) long. The Barrière Indians made a padding of canvas between the sleigh and the canoe. If it was a sleigh ordinarily pulled by dogs, the man would now pull it himself, as

he did not trust his dogs to pull his canoe.

Riding in a canoe, women sat flat, legs crossed, or on knees, sitting on feet. Men sat on feet or kneeled, rear end on the thwart.

When an Indian was guiding a white tourist, the tourist would be seated in front of the center thwart; otherwise, he would make too much noise when paddling.

Jim Jerome says that Indians were never worried about shooting rapids in a birchbark canoe.

Lina Nottaway recalls going in a 24-ft. birchbark canoe to Senneterre for food. They shot the rapids in the big canoe, a man with a long paddle in the stern and another man with a long paddle in the bow, both standing. They used to shout when they shot the rapids.

An old-style Algonquin birchbark canoe from the Ottawa River area, now in the collection of the National Museum of Denmark. The canoe, constructed in 1861, has a sheer that lies virtually flat except for an abrupt upswing just inboard of the bows. The lower part of the bow is more rounded than usual. (Photo courtesy Viking Ship Museum, Roskilde, Denmark.)

III

Jocko Carle, River Désert Algonquin, Maniwaki, Québec

Jocko Carle was a member of the River Désert Algonquin Band in Maniwaki, Québec. When the author spent time with him, in 1981, he was seventy-one years old and, along with his friend and fellow canoe builder Basil Smith, continued to be very active in trapping, guiding for fishing and hunting parties, and making birchbark canoes.

Basil was a slight man weighing about 50 kg (110 lbs.). He was in good health and was strong despite his weight and age, and carried his share of the load readily when unloading a canoe. He was a shy man and well known for his thoughtfulness. He worked most of the time for Désert Lake Fish and Game Club, about 60 km (40 mi.) northwest of Maniwaki, and was always sought after ahead of others for a hunting or fishing party, in great part because of his good humor.

Jocko Carle weighed 100 kg (220 lbs.) and was a strong man with much endurance, if not the speed he had when he was younger. Although the author had to slow down while walking on a road to wait for Jocko, the opposite was true in the woods. Jocko had a steady pace that lent itself quite well to managing the soft, tricky footing of the forest floor and the attendant ups and downs.

Jocko was noted for his energy, a drive that could keep him working on a canoe from six in the morning until eight at night and finish a canoe alone in seven days, probably the most efficient of all builders of the time. This enthu-

Jocko Carle and Basil Smith, River Désert Algonquin, at Round Lake, Québec, 1981. (Photo by David Gidmark.)

The first canoe made by Jocko Carle following a 37-year hiatus. Unlike most of Jocko's canoes, this one has a curved deck-piece instead of a flat one. (Photo by David Gidmark.)

The building bed behind Jocko Carle's house, River Désert Reserve. The two halves of the plywood building frame stand against the tree behind the bed. (Photo by David Gidmark, courtesy National Museums of Canada.)

Jocko Carle working with his crooked knife on sheathing for a birchbark canoe. (Photo by David Gidmark, courtesy National Museums of Canada.)

The Jocko Carle canoe used by the author on a 1979 trip along the Abitibi River towards James Bay. The canoe was 16 ft. long, had an outer beam measure of 37 in., and was 13 in. deep. (Photo by Bill Hambling.)

siasm at times exasperated Basil, who would prefer to take a break to smoke a pipe a little more often during the course of the day.

Jocko Carle was born one of sixteen children on Petawawagama Lake about 120 km (75 mi.) north of Maniwaki. Jocko's father, John Carle, was a well-known canoe maker and made canoes for sale, and one of Jocko's brothers, Peter, also became a canoe builder. Before the family moved onto the reserve in Maniwaki, they used more traditional tools and materials, such as a bone awl *(mîkos)* and sinew ("Indian thread") for sewing. The factor of distance had preserved the use of aboriginal tools in birchbark canoe making and other crafts into the 1930s and beyond.

In 1984 the author repaired a canoe apparently made by the Carle family from River Désert, likely in the 1930s. It had the nearly vertical bow of the Carle family, along with the flat bark deck-piece that Jocko favored. There were nails in the gunwales and gunwale caps. There was no broken rib at the bow, and it did not appear that there ever had been one, nor did the canoe have a headboard. Sheathing was haphazard. The stem-piece was lashed at the bottom with basswood bark. There was spruce root lashing on the side panel but none on the gores, nor were the bows lashed. The canoe was gummed with tar. Thwarts were lashed in with spruce root. Ribs narrowed in width as they went toward the bow. Sheer was typical of Jocko Carle's canoes, and the rocker was nearly straight.

As Jocko became more and more in demand as a guide during the early 1930s, he gave up canoe building for a long period, with the exception of one unusual circumstance during World War II.

About 1942, Jocko and another man were spring trapping with a canvas canoe. The rivers were open, but there was still a good deal of snow on the ground.

They had a lot of gear, plus fur and meat from a moose they had killed. Before heading back, they came upon a birch tree about 60 cm (2 ft.) in diameter. Thinking that it would be good to have another canoe, in view of all they were carrying, they set to work.

Because the ground was frozen and there was no reasonable way to get spruce root, they had to improvise. They used nails for the gunwales, and to bind the bows and lash the thwarts into the gunwales, they used *babiche* (hide) from the moose they had just killed. To get the bark off the tree—difficult in cold weather—they boiled water and ladled it over the bark as they removed it. In four days they had a good 4-m canoe and made their way back to Maniwaki.

Since the 1930s in Maniwaki, canoes were built rather infrequently, and prices did not rise very quickly. Peter Carle received only $125 for a canoe as recently as 1972. In the late 1970s, however, the price took a good upswing, and Basil suggested to Jocko that perhaps they should get building.

In the summer of 1979, Jocko and Basil set to work building a 4-m (13-ft.) canoe at one of Basil's trapping cabins on Rock Lake, north of Maniwaki in Parc de la Vérendrye. Their first effort was a commendable one, considering that Jocko had not done any significant canoe building for forty-five years and most of Basil's experience was as a helper. The canoe sold within days of their return for $600. With this encouragement, Jocko and Basil returned to Rock Lake to build two more canoes.

By 1981 their price for a canoe had gone up to $1,000. Jocko Carle's canoes can be found in the National Museum of Man; the Kanawa Museum in Minden, Ontario; and The Mariners' Museum in Newport News, Virginia.

To build the canoe for the National Museum of Man, Jocko and Basil went to a cabin on Round Lake, northwest of Maniwaki. This area had many of the raw materials they would need for the canoe close by.

To search out good birch bark (*wîkwâs*), Jocko, Basil, and the author put the axes, chain saw, and ropes in a boat and headed to a spot where Basil had seen some likely looking birch trees. There were indeed a number of large birches in the area, but it was difficult to find a good one; the bark would turn out to be too brittle or there would be some other problem, such as a slightly crooked trunk. Jocko is known in the Maniwaki band for having high standards regarding the quality of bark. He would test the bark by making an ax cut about 1.8 m (6 ft.) up from the base of the tree. He then tore off a small piece of bark and bent it back on itself to make sure that it was pliable enough to resist cracking. He also checked that

(Left) A Jocko Carle canoe at The Mariners' Museum in Newport News, Virginia. The canoe was purchased by the museum in 1983 from Kanawa Museum, Minden, Ontario, for $1,450. (Photo by David Gidmark.)

(Left) A canoe behind Jocko Carle's house. The scallops are done in winter bark, not by adding a scalloped piece of reinfor-cing bark (as is sometimes done). (Photo by David Gidmark, courtesy National Museums of Canada.)

(Above) A canoe made by Jocko Carle's brother Peter. The canoe displays the vertical bow typical of the Carle family. There is no head-board, and the sheathing is haphazard. (Photo by David Gidmark.)

A Carle family canoe from the 1930s. The gunwales were nailed, which may explain how the family managed to construct this full-sized canoe in four days. (Photo by David Gidmark, courtesy National Museums of Canada.)

An inboard view of the Carle family canoe from the 1930s. In later years, Jocko Carle's canoes rarely had head-boards. (Photo by David Gidmark, courtesy National Museums of Canada.)

Jocko Carle examining a bark sample, 1981. (Photo by David Gidmark.)

ward the bottom end of the tree, and the other just below the lowest branch. This way, when the birch log had to be moved, it could be rolled on these two logs.

Once the tree was downed, they sawed off the trunk just below the lowest branches, then made a cut along the top of the birch log deep enough to go through the bark to the wood. At this point, if a builder found that there was

the layers did not separate. The bark had to be of the right thickness as well. Jocko warned that it could occasionally be too thin at either the bottom or the top of the tree.

Finally Jocko found a tree that looked good after testing. The bark was of good quality, the trunk was straight, and the tree had a fortuitous lean, meaning that it would fall in a convenient direction. (Sometimes, despite the aid of a chain saw and experience, a tree gets hung up in the trees surrounding it and getting it to the ground is an enormous task.)

Jocko began to clear brush from around the trunk, and Basil prepared small trees that would be placed under the falling birch trunk to form a protective bed. Jocko walked leeward of the trunk to clear out the area where it would land. Then he suddenly began jumping up and down and quickly hopped off to one side. Indians have been known to chant or pray at certain stages of the canoe-building process, but I had witnessed Jocko gathering bark on many occasions and had never seen him perform a chant or a dance. But perhaps Jocko had for some reason decided this time to employ one. I dropped my ax and ran quickly for my notebook, intending to make notes and a sketch. It was only then that it became evident that Jocko had stepped into a bee's nest.

The nest precluded our working on the trunk any longer that day, so we headed back to the cabin. By chance that evening Jocko and Basil discovered a tree with suitable bark only 100 m (110 yds.) behind the cabin.

The next day, they removed the underbrush from the path of the trunk and cleared the ground of any stones or other obstructions that might damage the bark. Then they placed two logs crosswise for the trunk to fall on—one to-

Cutting a tree. (Photo by David Gidmark.)

Sawing a straight line through the bark of the downed birch is the first step. (Photo by David Gidmark, courtesy National Museums of Canada.)

a knot on an otherwise good section of bark, this cut could be made through the knot so that the bark would be rendered usable.

As it was a rather warm summer day, Jocko and Basil had only minor difficulty in peeling the bark. In colder weather it would be harder to get off. When they began to peel the bark, they used a 2.5-m (8-ft.) sapling that Basil had cut and cleared of branches. They pressed the sapling under the bark and against the trunk so that the peeling would proceed evenly. When they would reach a sticking point, they pried the bark away from the trunk with deft use of the ax blade or by poking with a wooden wedge.

Once the bark was off the tree (the sheet was a little over 4.5 m [15 ft.] long), they placed it on top of the trunk, carefully rolled it up white side in, and carried it back to camp. The roll was soaked in water overnight to make it more pliable. They would begin building the canoe the next morning. Jocko said that if the bark were good, it could be stored dry almost indefinitely and would need only to be soaked for a few days before use.

They cut white cedar along the shore of Round Lake. The long pieces for the gunwales (*pimikwanak*) were cut more than 4.5 m (15 ft.) long, as the final length of the canoe was to be 4 m (13 ft.). They felled the tree and split it into quarters lengthwise with hardwood wedges and a steel ax. Then Jocko trimmed it with the ax. He did much of this trimming before leaving the woods so that they would not be carrying useless weight back to camp. The same process was repeated for each rib piece (*wâginatik*), about 1.5 m (5 ft.) long. Jocko usually trimmed and split these so that blanks had only two ribs remaining in them.

An ax is used to peel the bark. (Photo by David Gidmark, courtesy National Museums of Canada.)

The spruce pole will be used to help remove the bark sheet evenly. (Photo by David Gidmark, courtesy National Museums of Canada.)

(Below left) "Spuds" of birchbark are another help in stripping the bark off the trunk. (Photo by David Gidmark, courtesy National Museums of Canada.)

(Below right) The spruce pole is laid under the bark, keeping the working area open. A sharp wooden wedge pries the bark from the tree. (Photo by David Gidmark.)

This not only reduced the weight he would have to carry back to the building site, but also allowed him to quickly check the quality of the potential ribs before investing additional effort in them.

Back at the building site the following day, Jocko carved all the ribs with his crooked knife while Basil prepared the spruce root *(watap).* He whittled down the rib blanks as far as possible to avoid extra work with the crooked

(Left) *The spruce roots, now soft and pliable, are split. Mosquitos account for Basil's beekeeping garb. (Photo by David Gidmark.)*

(Right) *The headboard blank is roughly cut with an ax. (Photo by David Gidmark, courtesy National Museums of Canada.)*

More precise carving on the headboard follows. (Photo by David Gidmark, courtesy National Museums of Canada.)

direction to bring the split back to center. Once he had split the blanks, there remained only a small amount of polishing to do.

He worked the crooked knife from the center of the ribs to the ends, tapering them in both thickness and width in the same direction. He made extra ribs in case he broke any during bending.

The gunwale members similarly were first shaved down with the ax and then split. Jocko

Jocko takes down the gunwale cap with the ax; he will finish it with a crooked knife. (Photo by David Gidmark, courtesy National Museums of Canada.)

knife *(mokotâgan)*. Occasionally he carved only one rib from a blank, but his usual practice was to carve two ribs as precisely as he could before splitting the blank.

He split the blanks from top end to butt end, starting the split with a large knife, and then working it with his hands. He kept the blank wedged between his knees, and if the split started to go off to one side, he pressed on the cedar with his knee in the opposite

ing root. Roots were gathered and then rolled up into an 8-kg (20-lb.) roll, tied, and brought back to camp, where Basil worked on them while Jocko carved ribs. Although work with the spruce root was ordinarily considered a woman's task, Jocko's wife was not interested in the project, so Basil, as the assistant, took on the duty.

Whenever he was not working on it, Basil kept the roll of spruce root in water to keep it as fresh as possible and to make the bark easier to remove.

He split the root by starting a small cut at

occasionally used two trees close together as a lever to aid in the splitting. He then finished them with the crooked knife.

Jocko and Basil had harvested spruce root from a clearing not too far from Fournier's Bay, Désert Lake. They would dig out from the base of the tree about 2 m (6 ft.) until they came to a root, often as much as 15 cm (6 in.) below the surface. The root was cut there and pulled out as far as possible. Some of the roots were as long as 6 m (20 ft.) or more. Often the root would cross under another, and the men would have to feed it under the obstruct-

Basil had earlier prepared a building bed down by the lake. He chose a spot that was heavily shaded so that sunlight would not dry out the bark. He cleared away all the underbrush and all rocks and roots from the ground where the bed was to be. He checked that the ground was sufficiently firm to hold the stakes that would go in later, and then he brought some bucketfuls of sand to build up the base. Jocko and Basil raked the bed together, and Jocko kept sighting it to see that it was as level as possible. Jocko planned to build a canoe with a straight rocker, so he wanted to have a level bed. The raked part of the bed was approximately 5 by 1.5 m (17 by 5 ft.). In re-

(Left top) The rib blank is rough-shaped with the ax, then carved to almost finished dimensions. (Photo by David Gidmark.)

(Left bottom) When split, the blank becomes two virtually finished ribs. (Photo by David Gidmark.)

The building bed, consisting of beach sand shoveled over the spaded forest floor, must be leveled before work begins. (Photo by David Gidmark.)

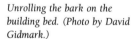

Unrolling the bark on the building bed. (Photo by David Gidmark.)

the thicker end and working it with his fingers toward the small end. If the split started going off to one side, he exerted pressure from the other to get it back to center. Once the root was split, he rolled it up in a small coil and put it in a pot of boiling water so that the thin bark would be easier to remove. After a few minutes, he took the root out, removed the bark, and quartered the root. Fully prepared roots were rolled into small coils again and put in water until later use.

Construction cannot begin until irregularities in the bark have been removed. (Photo by David Gidmark.)

The inwale assembly can function as a building frame. (Photo by David Gidmark, courtesy National Museums of Canada.)

Amid a pile of shavings, temporary thwarts are tied to the inwale assembly. (Photo by David Gidmark, courtesy National Museums of Canada.)

cent times a number of Algonquin builders have made building beds of planks set up off the ground, but Jocko has never done this.

The most efficient builders—and Jocko Carle must certainly rank near the top—had their materials well organized before beginning construction. All of the wooden members of the canoe—ribs, gunwales, and sheathing *(apisidaganik)*—had been prepared, and additional materials such as stakes, twine, and so on had been readied and were near at hand.

On the day that assembly was to begin, Jocko and Basil arose around 5:30. After a

hearty breakfast, Basil hurried down to the lake near the building site to start a fire. He filled a washtub with water and put it on the fire to boil.

The traditional Algonquin method of working with the hull form involves using the gunwale assembly as a building frame. In this method, the gunwale assembly is weighted down on the bark, the sides are turned up, and then later the gunwales are raised and fixed in their final position. This was also Jocko's traditional method, and the one that he had used most often in the old days. He had recently found, however, that he preferred to use a two-piece plywood building frame.

Basil and Jocko chose a spot in the center of the building bed, made sure it was free of bumps, and placed the two halves of the plywood frame on the ground. They drove birch stakes about 75 cm (2½ ft.) long and 4 cm (1½ in.) in diameter into the ground next to the frame, in pairs on opposite sides of the frame. The stakes were spaced about 50 cm (20 in.) apart. The spacing was somewhat closer toward the bows.

They checked once more that everything was lined up properly. Satisfied of the placement, they carefully removed each stake and laid it to the side, beyond where the bark would rest on the bed but directly out from the hole. After this, they removed the building frame. Then they examined the building bed once again, seeing that there were still no imperfections and that the stake holes formed a symmetrical pattern where the building frame had been.

(Left) *The building frame is carefully positioned on the bark. (Photo by David Gidmark, courtesy National Museums of Canada.)*

Next, they rolled the bark out on the bed white side up. They examined the white side closely to make sure that there were no serious blemishes, pulled off loose pieces of bark, and scraped small blemishes smooth with a knife. This was done so that there would be no unevenness in the finished hull.

When the white side of the bark was clean, it was centered carefully over the stake hole pattern, and then the building frame was centered on the bark. The men had gathered several heavy stones, totaling about 200 kg (450 lbs.), from around the lake area; these were now placed on the frame to weight it down.

Basil brought boiling water from the fire and ladled it over the bark around the outside of the building frame, particularly at each bow, where the bark would have to undergo the sharpest bending. Then they turned up the bark all around the building frame until the stake holes were visible. As the bark was turned up, they reinserted the stakes in their holes, planted them firmly in the ground with a mallet, and tied together the tops of each pair with a cord.

Gores are often cut into the sides of the canoe while the bark is still flat on the ground. Jocko, however, cut them in the bark just after it was turned up and the stakes tied in pairs, reasoning that after the bark was turned up, folds in the side would show more clearly where gores were actually needed.

He cut each gore in a straight line down to the building frame. The cut was made on a diagonal through the bark so that a bevel was created on each edge. When the edges were overlapped, the bevels were hidden from the outside view. The gores were overlapped in the same direction from the bow of the canoe to

Hundreds of pounds of rocks and bricks must be loaded on top of the building frame. (Photo by David Gidmark, courtesy National Museums of Canada.)

Battens are placed on the outboard edges, for support. (Photo by David Gidmark, courtesy National Museums of Canada.)

Around the plywood form weighted with stones, the sides of the canoe are brought up and held up by stakes. (Photo by David Gidmark.)

(Left) *A gore is cut in the side panel. (Photo by David Gidmark.)*

(Right) *The bark will crack and split if it is worked dry; pouring hot water helps keep it pliable as the bow is formed. (Photo by David Gidmark, courtesy National Museums of Canada.)*

(Below) *The inwales, still held in position with their temporary thwarts, are fit into the canoe. (Photo by David Gidmark, courtesy National Museums of Canada.)*

A side panel is cut with the aid of a straightedge. (Photo by David Gidmark, courtesy National Museums of Canada.)

the stern, so that there would be less resistance as the canoe floated through the water. Although Jocko sometimes stitched the gores, he usually would leave them to be held in place by being sandwiched between the inwale and outwale.

Once the sides were up and the gores cut, the men added an extra piece of bark to each side of the canoe to fill out the beam. These pieces were about 1.5 m (5 ft.) long and were fitted inboard of the sides and down to the edge of the building frame. The men made sure that the eyes of the added bark pieces went in the same direction as those in the main piece. An uneven edge was left on the main bark where the extra piece was added, and Jocko would trim this off later with a small knife.

As soon as the side pieces were in position, Basil began to sew them into place. He used a straightedge to make a guideline in pencil for the length of the sewing, and a steel-bladed awl to make holes through the double thickness of the bark. These holes were spaced about 2.5 cm (1 in.) apart.

Basil then looked through the spruce roots he had prepared for one that was long, even, and sturdy. He put the root halfway through the first hole, and then laced the root halves to cross each other at the holes until the job was finished. At the end, he brought the out-

low. The top ends were all tied with cord to the outside stakes with which they were paired, thereby helping to hold the inwale assembly and the outwale tightly in place.

To aid in fairing the sides, the men fitted wooden battens between pairs of stakes. These were thin sheets of cedar that actually were discarded pieces of sheathing.

Jocko and Basil next cut the excess bark down to the gunwales. Making occasional small adjustments so that the gunwales were well placed, they then clamped the gunwales together tightly using iron C-clamps. These clamps were placed so that the roots would later hide the marks that the clamps inevitably would leave in the soft cedar. Some builders made tongues in the bark to overlap at the root sites, feeling that this gave added strength by not allowing the inwales to ride up when the ribs were forced into place. Jocko occasionally made these tongues, but he felt that it did not make that great a difference and more often, as on this canoe, opted not to make them.

Preparatory to the sewing of the gunwales, the inwale and the outwale had to be pegged. Jocko made dowels about 1 cm (³/₈ in.) in diameter and 20 cm (8 in.) long from dry birch. Although many Algonquin builders used square pegs, Jocko found that round ones worked better for him.

He drilled holes with a hand drill through the gunwales at every other root lashing, put the dowels through the holes, and pounded them in until they would go no farther. He and Basil then sawed each peg (mitikötcitahaskwan) off flush with the gunwales. The spruce root would later hide these pegs.

While Jocko attended to some other work, Basil began the long chore of sewing the gunwales with the spruce root. In the construction of the Algonquin canoe, this was traditionally woman's work. In the 1930s, when Jocko had last built many canoes, his sister had helped him and his father and brother. Now, in his building of canoes during the last three years, Basil usually took on the chore, although Jocko did the spruce root work himself on some of his recent canoes. His and Basil's sewing styles differed somewhat.

Basil pulled a coil of finished spruce root from the lake as he needed it. His original 8-kg (20-lb.) doughnut had been prepared into many coils, and these he had only to pull out

board root halfway through the last hole by itself and tied an overhand knot with the inboard root half.

Then the men were ready to fit the inwale assembly into the canoe. They placed measuring sticks with little shoulders on them under the inwale at the intermediate and the center thwarts. Jocko wanted to keep the depth at these sites the same so that in the finished canoe, the sheer between these points in the midsection of the canoe would have as little rise as possible.

While the inwale assembly was standing temporarily in place, the men placed the outwales at the same height outboard of the bark and next to the stakes. Then they put small stakes that had been cut earlier inside of the inwale and paired with each outside stake. The smaller stakes had a bevel at the bottom end; this pried against the building frame be-

The inwale and outwale are clamped together while the gunwale is adjusted to its proper height. (Photo by David Gidmark.)

The bow is pressed into shape. The ends of the outwales have not yet been raised to their final height. (Photo by David Gidmark.)

the men achieved a graceful sheer upsweep that began near the intermediate thwart.

When all the sewing had been done beyond the last thwarts on both ends, Basil and Jocko removed the two halves of the plywood building frame and several large rocks that were weighting it down. They would not have been able to do this had not there been temporary, removable thwarts in the inwale assembly. When the temporary thwarts were untied and the frame and rocks taken out, the permanent ash *(akimâk)* thwarts *(pîmitisak,* pl.) could be placed into the inwale.

At each thwart site, a mortise was cut using a small screwdriver and a hammer. The mortise went through the inwale to the bark. The location for the mortise had been traced with the end of the thwart, and this end was placed against the mortise as it was being fashioned to check for the proper size.

When the thwart was fitted into the mortise, it was lashed in much the same way as the sewing along the gunwale, except that the spruce root was passed through the three holes near the end of the thwart instead of simply around the inwale. The root was passed two or three times through each hole as necessary. These holes were made with a hand drill, but

one at a time as he needed them. From a coil he took the 2-m (6-ft.) lengths he needed to sew at a single site.

He made four or five holes immediately under the outwale with a triangular-bladed awl. The root was anchored in the sandwich of the outwale and the bark, through a little hole made with the awl. The root was wrapped tightly around the gunwale and bark and passed two times through each hole. When the site was finished, the root end was pulled back under the last two strands on the top of the gunwale. In this way, both the start and the finish of the root sewing would later be hidden by the gunwale cover. The inwale assembly still contained the dummy thwarts; when Basil came to a thwart, he skipped over it.

As the sewing passed beyond the intermediate thwarts, Jocko raised the inwale assembly. The gunwales had been rather level through the midsection of the canoe, and the sheer now became evident. He liked to raise the inwale assembly at this time because he felt that the sewing throughout the midsection of the gunwales held the assembly in place better and held the straight sheer that he wanted to achieve along the midsection.

He and Basil raised the inwale assembly slightly, and one site was sewn on the port side and one on the starboard side. The assembly was raised again, and two more sites were sewn, and so on until the sewing had passed the end thwart and neared the bow. In this way

Jocko used to make them with only a steel awl and some elbow grease. Although some Algonquin builders put a peg through the inwale and the thwart end, Jocko did not on this canoe.

At this point, with the permanent thwarts lashed into the canoe, the building frame and rocks taken out, and the gunwale sewn to a point close to the bows, the canoe was raised onto two carpenter's horses and turned upside down. Jocko and Basil ladled hot water over the bow preparatory to cutting it to the final bow profile. Jocko cut the bark from the tip of the bow to the bottom of the canoe; this was important, because if he cut in the opposite direction, he might have caught the grain of the bark, resulting in a tear. He constantly tried the stem-piece *(wåginawinj)* in the bow of the canoe to make sure that the bow profile was conforming to it.

The heel of the stem-piece was forced firmly against the bottom of the inner hull and then clamped into place. Basil and Jocko worked together to drill holes through the stem-piece and two sheets of bark. One held the bow while the other drilled with a hand drill. They put the holes approximately through the middle of the stem-piece.

The bow was sewn with a double cross-stitch from a point just below the tip of the bow to the point where the bow began its curve; then it changed to a double in-and-out stitch. The finishing of the top part of the bow—where the gunwale met the stem-piece—was left for later.

Before they put the canoe back on the building bed, the men again smoothed out the bed. The next step was to bend the ribs, and Jocko wanted to make sure that the bark would be resting on a smooth surface while the hull was being formed. He went to the lake and fished a bunch of ribs from the water.

Basil now had to stoke a roaring fire so that the washtub full of water would be kept boiling to bend the ribs. He also had to sweep out the bottom of the canoe and remove any remaining blemishes on the inner bark that could conveniently be gotten out.

Jocko placed some pieces of sheathing in the bottom of the canoe. These were temporary pieces that would be placed under the ribs only to give the approximate depth of the later permanent sheathing. These were pieces of

Sweeping out the canoe before the next step: bending the ribs. The crosspieces have been nailed across the gunwales to resist outboard pressure from the drying ribs. (Photo by David Gidmark.)

The sheathing—at this point tapered only at one end—and the ribs are ready. (Photo by David Gidmark.)

sheathing that had been discarded from earlier projects as imperfect but that served this purpose.

The day the ribs were bent was the most concentrated, in terms of energy, of the entire project. While most Algonquin builders looked forward with trepidation toward the bending of the ribs, Jocko did even more so. Ribs break, and Jocko's had more of a tendency than most to break, as they were somewhat thicker than the usual ribs. This time, he was armed with a dozen or so additional ribs, so he felt protected somewhat, but one never really knows.

From the bunch of finished ribs that he had taken from the water, Jocko selected two of the

Jocko Carle at sunrise, pouring boiling water down the length of a pair of ribs to facilitate bending. (Photo by David Gidmark.)

The rib is bent in two places only, to form the bilges. (Photo by David Gidmark, courtesy National Museums of Canada.)

To hold each rib in place while it dries, Basil drives a nail through it into the inwale. (Photo by David Gidmark, courtesy National Museums of Canada.)

greatly. If this happened, it meant either that the rib was still too thick, in which case he thinned it more with his crooked knife, or that it needed more steaming in the boiling water. He bent two ribs at a time because one supported the other and they were less likely to break in tandem.

When the first pair of ribs was bent sufficiently, Jocko held them by the tops and carried them to the canoe. With the temporary sheathing in place, he inserted them in the first rib site immediately next to the center thwart. He pushed the ribs down so that they were as snug as possible against the bottom of the canoe, and then removed the inner rib and put it in the next rib site alongside the first rib. Jocko turned one rib of each pair around after he bent them. This would equalize the pressure that the ribs exerted and make for a symmetrical hull. To hold the ribs in place for drying, Jocko simply put a nail through each rib and into the gunwale. This left a nail hole in the inwale later, but it was significantly easier than waiting to anchor the ribs later when the binder would be inserted.

The bending continued with good results; only a few ribs were broken, and they were

widest. He took them to the tub of boiling water and ladled water over them for three or four minutes, holding the two of them together and covering the entire ribs with water, but particularly the two spots where the bends were to occur. When they were sufficiently heated, he brought them back to a bench, sat down, and started the bend by working the two ribs back and forth over his knee slowly past the spot where the bend was to be. As he slowly bent the two ribs, Jocko watched that the cedar did not resist too

replaced by the extras that Jocko had made. When the ribs were all bent and nailed into place temporarily, Jocko and Basil put the binder in the canoe. The binder is similar to a couple of dummy gunwales that are to be wedged apart by crosspieces. The purpose of the binder is to form the ribs, and therefore the hull shape of the canoe. The ribs are forced into roughly a lying C position, the bottom relatively flat. The binder is forced out by the tightly wedged crosspieces and is forced down by wedging small lengths of wood under the thwarts.

Once the binder is in the canoe, it exerts tremendous pressure on the hull. Braces must be put across the top of the canoe to hold things together. When Jocko began to make canoes a few years ago after his long hiatus, this fact had slipped his mind. He had put the binder in and placed the canoe in the sun to dry the ribs. When he came out the next morning, the gunwales had spread apart, tearing the lashed-in thwarts from the mortises. It was an effective memory jogger.

After the braces were nailed across the gunwales, the canoe was propped in the sun so that the ribs would dry. It was left for two days, during which time some other finishing work was done. Jocko also took advantage of the time to begin working on some ribs for another canoe and to make some designs on the canoe. These could be made at almost any time after the ribs gave rigidity to the hull, and were indeed most often made when all other work was done.

Jocko wet the bark by ladling some warm water over the hull, where he had placed some empty potato sacks. After five or ten minutes of soaking, the dark brown rind was soft

enough to be scraped. He did the scraping with a dull knife. He used a fish figure, plus a scallop design under the gunwales. On other canoes he had sometimes added moose silhouettes.

When the ribs were dry enough for their final placement in the canoe, Basil and Jocko again smoothed the building bed and replaced the canoe right side up. They knocked the binder supports from the canoe and took out the nails holding the rib tops to the gunwales.

Basil again swept the inside hull of the canoe to make sure that it was clean, then gummed the seams on the inside of the hull. Meanwhile, Jocko examined pieces of the permanent sheathing to select ones for the inside of the canoe.

The binders are fitted into the canoe, temporarily held in place with struts. They push against the ribs while the canoe maker adjusts the fit of the ribs. When snug, the ribs are cut flush with the gunwales. (Photo by David Gidmark, courtesy National Museums of Canada.)

The binder struts are knocked out. (Photo by David Gidmark, courtesy National Museums of Canada.)

The sewn seams inside the canoe are gummed with pine rosin. (Photo by David Gidmark, courtesy National Museums of Canada.)

(Left) Jocko Carle sorts pieces of sheathing for the inside. (Photo by David Gidmark, courtesy National Museums of Canada.)

(Right) The first piece of sheathing fits snugly under the end of the stem-piece. (Photo by David Gidmark.)

With all the sheathing in place, the ribs are pounded into the canoe. (Photo by David Gidmark.)

Although the ribs were bent and inserted to dry in the canoe from the center thwart to the bow, they would be wedged under the inwale starting from the bow and working toward the center thwart.

Jocko placed the first piece of sheathing next to the heel of the stem-piece. This piece of sheathing must be a flexible one, because it had to bend with the sharp fold of the bark at this point. Although he sometimes attempted to fit the end of the piece of cedar sheathing under the heel of the stem-piece, in this canoe he chose to make a notch in the cedar into which the end of the stem-piece could fit snugly.

Once the first piece of sheathing was securely fitted in place, other pieces were added going up to the gunwale on each side, so that the bark was completely covered. Jocko quickly made a bevel in the rib nearest the bow; he wedged it in temporary fashion so that it would hold the pieces of sheathing in place while the other nearby ribs were being readied.

To cut off a rib to the desired length, Jocko first pushed the rib to the bottom of the canoe and noted the spot where each end of the rib was even with the top of the gunwale. Then he removed the rib and, with the crooked knife, made bevels at that point and on each side of the rib end, so that the rib end was beveled on three sides.

He took the rib back to the canoe and inserted the beveled ends under the inwale at a point between the two spruce root lashings. To drive it into place, he used a hammer along with a wooden driving stick to protect the soft cedar from hammer marks.

When a rib is forced into position, it exerts considerable pressure. It is this pressure by all the ribs in concert, along with the general strength of the materials, that makes the hull of the birchbark canoe so strong and solid. The birchbark canoe is not the flimsy craft it is so often portrayed to be in the popular literature.

Jocko and Basil did not pound the ribs home to a directly vertical position in the canoe, but rather left them all about 5 cm (2 in.) short of the vertical. Jocko did this to allow the

bark time to give under the increasing pressure of the ribs. About two hours later, he and Basil hammered home the ribs to the vertical.

The gunwale cap (*apatapikåhigan*) was a long piece of cedar resembling one of the gunwales. It was longer than a gunwale to begin with (it would later be shortened to finish properly at the bows) and slightly narrower than the gunwale-bark sandwich when viewed from above. According to Jocko, its function was to protect the spruce root lashing when the canoe was in use.

The cap was first centered lengthwise at the center thwart. Basil held it tightly to the gunwale while Jocko drilled a hole on either side of the center thwart through the cap and the inwale. Then Basil inserted a long, round peg in both holes. He bent the gunwale cap slightly to conform to the curve of the gunwale just after each peg was added.

The pegs were put through the cap at alternate rib sites. When they were all in tightly, they were sawn off flush with the gunwale above and below.

Jocko next carefully bent the ends of the gunwale cap to follow the sheer toward the bow. There was some resistance to the bending of the cap on a couple of occasions, and Jocko had to thin the cedar sufficiently with his crooked knife.

The end of the gunwale cap narrows substantially toward the bow, so that it would be

difficult to put a peg through it without splitting it. Therefore, spruce root is lashed around the gunwale and the gunwale cap at the same site, in order to hold the cap in place.

The men then had to shave off the ends of the gunwales and the caps just beyond the stem-piece. These pinch the stem-piece as they are all lashed together just inboard of the stem-piece. A thick piece of birch bark that is left flat and is sandwiched between the gunwale cap and the gunwale serves to cover the small bow. On this model, it did not extend down below the outwales, although Jocko has made some that did. This deck-piece is typical of both Jocko and John Carle's canoes. Adney suggested that this piece of bark was called *wulegissis* by some tribes.

For a sealing compound, Jocko used a commercial pine rosin. He reasoned, with com-

mendable logic, that it was far less time-consuming to do this than to traipse through the woods and located wounded spruce trees from which spruce gum (*pikiw*) could be gathered.

While the bark is adjusting to the pressure of the ribs, Jocko puts the cap on the gunwale and clamps it in place. (Photo by David Gidmark, courtesy National Museums of Canada.)

The outwale broke as it was being raised to the peak of the stem. After it was spliced and resewn, one could hardly tell where the break had occurred. The vertical stem is characteristic of Carle canoes. (Photo by David Gidmark.)

To soften the bark for scraping, wet potato sacks are draped on the canoe. (Photo by David Gidmark, courtesy National Museums of Canada.)

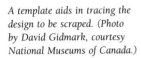

A template aids in tracing the design to be scraped. (Photo by David Gidmark, courtesy National Museums of Canada.)

he added lard little by little to increase the rosin's viscosity until he was sure that it was of the proper consistency—not so brittle that it would later crack too easily, and not so thin that it would run in the hot sun. He tested the gum by taking the stirring stick from the pot and seeing if the dripping stream would break. If so, he would add more lard. Jocko left no doubt as to how he was able to judge the delicate balance that would indicate an effective mixture of rosin and lard. "Experience," he said.

He applied the sealer to all the seams with a wooden spatula, applying it directly to the sewing on the bow without any strip of material being added over the stitching, as was sometimes done on the Algonquin canoes. It covered the unsewn gores along the sides, the sewn seam where the extra piece of bark had been added along the side, and the bow on each end. When the sealer had to be worked into place, Jocko and Basil wet their thumbs so that it would not stick to them.

When all was ready, Jocko and Basil carried the canoe down to the lake for a try and for some pictures. They were well satisfied with

Now finished, the bow is decorated with a fish design. Note the flat bark deck-piece, which Jocko often favored. (Photo by David Gidmark.)

it, and it did not require any further gumming. At the author's suggestion, another man was added to the load. With the three aboard, the little 4-m (13-ft.) canoe was carrying about 240 kg (530 lb.) with about 7 to 10 cm ($2^3/4$ to 4 in.) of freeboard, which serves to illustrate the carrying capacity of the birchbark canoe.

Back on shore, the canoe was again turned upside down on the carpenter's horses, and Jocko and Basil looked over the hull, satisfied with their work. The author, admiring the solidity of the rib work and the resiliency of the bark, inquired of Jocko how long the canoe could be expected to last. He turned to the author and responded explicitly, "Forever!"

The canoe is tight and handles well in the water. A scallop design is visible in the midsection, just below the gunwale. (Photo by David Gidmark, courtesy National Museums of Canada.)

IV

William Commanda, River Désert Algonquin, Maniwaki, Québec

The following chapter was recorded by the author in 1979.

William and Mary Commanda live near Maniwaki, Québec, 130 km (80 mi.) north of Ottawa. They are members of the River Désert Algonquin Band. William was chief of the band from 1951 to 1970.

William and Mary Commanda have been making several birchbark canoes a year for a number of years. Birchbark canoes were much a part of the childhood of both, although William's father was not a canoe maker, as Mary's was. She learned much of canoe-making technique from her father, Charlie Smith, who worked on canoes almost up to the time he died at age ninety-four.

William says that in 1925, when there were 325 Indians in the River Désert Band, there were more than twenty canoe makers, the best known among them being Pete Dubé and Charlie Commanda. Now there are about 1,000 Indians in the River Désert Band, but William, Basil Smith, and Jocko Carle have been the only active canoe makers in recent years.

In 1975 William and Mary taught a class of fifteen Algonquin students in Amos, Québec, in the craft and art of making birchbark canoes. They divided the students into two groups, each of them heading one. One would go into the woods for two or three days, while the other would stay with the second group and teach a part of the process. They made twelve canoes that summer, ranging in length from 3 to 5 m. They wanted to make canoes of different lengths to give the students a wider experience. "They already knew a lot about building," William says. "I knew because of the way they handled the crooked knives. They came with their own crooked knives."

The Commandas constructed a canoe in Washington, D.C., in 1976 during the Bicentennial celebration. They began it in Maniwaki and finished it in front of the Washington Monument. William maintains that "we only went there to demonstrate the making of a canoe. I didn't go to celebrate someone else's bicentennial."

In 1981 they went to Roskilde, Denmark, where they constructed a canoe at the Viking Ship Museum.

Western Québec and the Maniwaki region are good areas for birch bark (*wíkwás*). William

61

and Mary make several forays into the woods each year to look for birch bark and other canoe materials. Probably the hardest part of constructing a birchbark canoe is gathering the materials—in particular, knowing where and how to gather them. Not too many years ago, they could merely walk back in the woods several miles from town and get all the bark and wood they needed for a canoe. Eventually, though, because of logging and the fact that so many builders took bark from the area, good birch bark became hard to find. Now the Commandas must go as far as 150 km (90 mi.) into the woods to obtain the bark.

William Commanda tests a sample of birch bark for suppleness by bending it against the "eyes." (Photo by David Gidmark.)

When the Commandas go into the woods, they pack up their camper truck and sometimes stay the night, sometimes return the same day. William drives along a bush road until he spots the top of a large birch tree. Usually he returns to an area he has already visited and where he knows there are good birch trees. He parks the truck and gathers his gear for the walk back to the tree to examine it. At a minimum, he and Mary take a saw, a couple of axes to peel the bark, and a tumpline to wrap it up and carry it.

To build a 4-m (13-ft.)birchbark canoe, William looks for a tree that has a minimum diameter of 40 cm (15 in.) at the butt, but even that does not guarantee that the sheet of bark will be wide enough. He and Mary often have to sew smaller pieces on each side to increase the width.

There are also other things to consider. Just because the tree is large enough doesn't mean it is suitable for canoe building. The trunk has to be fairly straight, or else when the longitudinal cut is made on the bark, the sheet will be twisted and unusable. Any knots that might be hidden in the bark would inevitably show up later in the canoe as bumps.

After making sure the trunk is straight, the bark has to be tested. William taps the ax blade into the bark at a lower level and takes off a small piece of bark to examine it. For use in a canoe, birch bark must be a minimum of 3 mm ($^1/_8$ in.) thick. Strangely, it would be possible to find a large-diameter birch tree whose bark was too thin.

Besides checking the thickness of the bark, William makes sure the bark is not diseased, and he also tests it for pliability. Birch bark is made up of a number of layers. In healthy bark, these layers stay together. If the bark is of poor quality, the layers separate, and the bark must be rejected. The test for this is simply to bend the piece of bark back and forth. When healthy bark is folded outside in, it resists cracking. There is one type of bark, called red bark (*miskwa wîkwâs*), that resembles winter bark but is very prone to cracking.

Before he fells the tree, William makes a solid bed on which the tree can land. This bed

is a cradle of small trees placed a little above the point where the lower branches of the birch will fall. If the trunk of the birch tree is not thus prevented from hitting the ground as it falls, it may hit a rock or a tree stump, which would damage the bark.

In prehistoric times, it was hard to fell a tree. Fire was used to accomplish the task. The Indian first applied wet mud around the bark he wished to preserve. Then he built a good fire at the base of the trunk. When the wood below the mud was charred, he chopped away the burnt part with a crude stone ax. He repeated the steps until he had cut through the trunk entirely.

Once William and Mary have felled the tree, they make a cut about 12 mm ($^1/_2$ in.) deep—just deep enough to cut through the bark—from the base of the trunk to the spot where the branches begin. From that point they try to peel the bark evenly along the trunk's entire length. A hand is pushed between the bark and the tree to help remove the bark. Sometimes a dull-pointed wooden wedge is used to pry it off, and a stick about 3 m (10 ft.) long may be rolled against the trunk to ensure that the bark comes off evenly.

The bark is rolled inside out. A tumpline makes it easier to carry the roll from the woods. (Photo by David Gidmark.)

If the cutting is done on a warm day, the bark comes off easily. In colder weather, the bark is much harder to remove. Then, special care has to be taken to avoid tearing the bark. Sometimes, especially in winter, boiling water would have to be applied to the trunk before the bark could be peeled.

When the bark is off, it is one large sheet perhaps 5 m (16 ft.) long and 1.4 m (4¹/₂ ft.) wide, the size varying according to the size of the tree. This sheet is rolled up with the outside (the white side) of the bark on the inside of the roll. The roll is then tied with a tumpline and carried off.

William and Mary try to get winter bark (*pipon wíkwâs*) when they can. They generally decorate their canoes with beavers and moose by applying a stencil to the winter bark, and then scraping off the surrounding moist bark, leaving a dark figure on the hull.

Birch bark is a light, watertight, and wonderfully resilient material. It is still pliable when removed from the tree, but it dries within days, becoming hard and brittle to a certain degree. It is invariably in the roll by this time, and it can be saved for many months if stored in the proper place. The bark must be completely soaked for days before it regains its pliability. A birchbark canoe that is in the water from time to time is a healthy canoe; the bark absorbs a little water and can "breathe" again.

For a fastener, the only thing that holds a birchbark canoe together is lashing with spruce root. This root is fairly easy to gather, but in its preparation and lashing it represents perhaps one-third of the time involved in building a birchbark canoe.

To get spruce root, William and Mary go to a place 160 km (100 mi.) northeast of Maniwaki. Here, 10-m (35-ft.) spruce trees grow in fairly open areas. These trees have long roots that are not entangled with the roots of surrounding underbrush—but that doesn't mean that they are not entangled with each other.

Mary goes a few feet out from the trunk of the spruce tree and digs down with a dull-pointed stick, which will get through the dirt without damaging the roots. When she locates a good root, she tears out its whole length, which often approaches 6 m (20 ft.). Ideal root is the diameter of a pencil. Often the root on which she is tugging crosses under another root, in which case she feeds it under. She will work on this other root when she finishes with the first.

When she has a number of roots piled up, she rolls them up into a doughnut and ties the roll. This doughnut, weighing about 10 km (20 lbs.), can then be carried out of the woods conveniently.

William and Mary seal the very few parts of the canoe that are not watertight with spruce

The spruce roots, some of them quite long, are tied in bundles. (Photo by David Gidmark.)

A knife cut starts the split in the root. (Photo by David Gidmark.)

The root is then pulled apart by hand. (Photo by David Gidmark, courtesy National Museum of the American Indian, Smithsonian Institution.)

Boiling water helps remove the bark from the roots. (Photo by David Gidmark, courtesy National Museum of the American Indian, Smithsonian Institution.)

A roll of watap is ready for use. (Photo by David Gidmark, courtesy National Museum of the American Indian, Smithsonian Institution.)

gum (*pikiw*). In the spring, when the sap flows up the trees, they can collect the spruce gum in nearly the same way as maple sap. At other times of the year, they have to scrape it laboriously from wounds in spruce trees.

To get cedar for ribs, gunwales, and sheathing, William goes about 120 km (75 mi.) west of the place where he and Mary harvested the spruce root. Proper cedar for ribs and sheathing is not difficult to find. William needs longs only 3.5 m (12 ft.) in length or so.

White cedar is notoriously knotty and its grain twisty. A finished rib should not have a knot in it, as the wood curves around even a small knot. Wood with twisted grain will not split straight.

What is hard to come by, though, is the fine, straight, long cedar log needed for the gunwales. Here, the search is akin to the search for good bark. A builder could search among hundreds of white cedars before finding one with a knot-free trunk, bark indicating a straight grain, and a length of 5 m (16 ft.).

William has a favorite stand of cedar another 160 km (100 mi.) or so back in the woods. He approaches a likely tree, puts his hand on the trunk, and walks around it once or twice, head upraised to examine the trunk. If the tree passes his scrutiny, he fells it and cuts off a 5-m (16-ft.) long log just below the branches. He splits the log in half and then quarters using steel and hardwood wedges and a 2-kg (5-lb.) hammer or an ax. If the quarters are of medium size, they might yield four gunwales—enough for one canoe. From two or three big cedar trunks, William can stock up on enough long cedar to make many canoes.

Before construction of the canoe begins, the materials have to be prepared. The big roll of birch bark is submerged in water for a few days so that it will be pliable. If it is not soaked, it becomes so brittle that it is unusable.

The preparation of the spruce root is simple but time-consuming. The root is also soaked for a time so that it will be easier to work with. Then a split is started at one end of the root with a little knife cut. The root is evenly split for its length. If the split starts to run to one side, the other root half is pulled until the split evens up.

The spruce root has bark that must be removed, and boiling is sometimes necessary to

(Left) *Gunwales start out as a quarter-sawn log. Splitting the log with iron wedges gets the canoe maker closer to gunwale size. (Photo by David Gidmark.)*

(Right) *To split ribs, William carefully applies leverage with his knees, bringing the split back to center if it goes off to one side. (Photo by David Gidmark.)*

(Left) *Finishing a rib is done on a shaving horse, with a drawknife. Most Indians used the crooked knife. (Photo by David Gidmark, courtesy National Museum of the American Indian, Smithsonian Institution.)*

(Right) *The crooked knife is an old Indian tool. This example belonged to William Commanda. (Photo by David Gidmark.)*

facilitate this. A good time to do this is after the root has been split in half. It is then easily peeled off with the thumbnail. There are often tiny branches on the root, which should be removed at this time as well.

Once this length of root is split all the way, both halves are sometimes split again to get rid of the middle of the root, a coarser fiber. After a long root is split, it is again rolled into a coil. It can then be left to dry if desired and soaked once again before use.

For William and Mary's construction of a canoe, the old Indian tools suffice in most cases. William splits the cedar gunwales, ribs, and sheathing by hand, because the split is stronger if it follows the grain. He has five or six crooked knives and about the same number of drawknives. These two hand tools are

no longer common, but they are extremely useful.

The drawknife is an old settler's tool. It is nothing more than a straight blade with handles on each end, perpendicular to the blade. The carver pulls the blade toward himself. This used to very often be employed for taking bark from logs. William uses it to make paddles and snowshoe frames and for finishing gunwales, ribs, and sheathing after they have been split, although most Algonquin used crooked knives for the latter operations. It is not easy to use a drawknife at first, but those who take the time to learn to use it swear by it. The beginner has a tendency to pull the knife toward him so that the blade is at right angles to the line of pull; the correct method is to pull the knife in a straight line but with the blade at an angle. The cutting is smoother this way. The carver also needs to take time to become sensitive to each movement of the blade in order to work with precision.

The crooked knife is an old Indian tool. Its appearance and method of use roughly approximate those of a hunting knife that would be pulled toward the carver. The handle is bent away, however, so that the thumb can be braced against it. The blade is slightly curved. The knife is pulled toward the carver because

The ends of the ribs are tapered after they have been bent in the canoe and are dry. (Photo by David Gidmark, courtesy National Museum of the American Indian, Smithsonian Institution.)

this action, as in the case of the drawknife, gives more control. The crooked knife also requires practice, but once the carver has become accustomed to it, he finds this a very useful tool. It is also more versatile than the drawknife, being able to carve in close spots.

The crooked knife is closely associated with Indian tradition. In the Maniwaki area, there are a number of Indians and a number of white men who make ax handles and paddles. Interestingly, despite long years of association with each other, the white men invariably use the drawknife for this work while the Indians use the crooked knife.

The inwales are marked at two-inch intervals. Spruce root lashings will be wrapped over the Xs, and the rib ends will fit in between. (Photo by David Gidmark.)

In aboriginal times, canoe-making tools were much more primitive. Holes in the bark were made with a triangular bone awl. Holes in wood were made using a type of awl with a bow that made it rotate. This looked much like the assembly Indians used for making a fire. And when the ribs were split, they were finished by means of abrasion, not by cutting as is done today. Indians used stones or shells to wear down the ribs, gunwales, and sheathing to proper form. Whatever the tools used, the Indian built craft of remarkable workmanship, even in prehistoric times.

The temporary center thwart will remain tied to the inwale assembly until the permanent thwart is inserted later in the construction process. (Photo by David Gidmark.)

William and Mary use a building platform rather than a canoe bed on the ground. In the last century or so, building platforms have become more common, as they allow several

To shape the building frame, a flexible cedar batten is bent on a 4 by 8 ft. plywood sheet and traced.

canoes to be constructed with a minimum of inconvenience.

A building platform is made by joining boards together. This platform is about 1.2 m (4 ft.) wide and about 5 m (16 ft.) long, depending on the size of the canoe. Building a canoe on a platform rather than on the ground has no effect on the form or structure of the finished canoe.

William sets his platform up on carpenter's horses so that it will not be necessary to kneel down while working on the canoe. He drills holes in the platform to receive the stakes that hold up the sides of the canoe. These holes are placed along the gunwale line about a foot and a half apart, in pairs directly opposite one another.

After William and Mary have soaked the roll of bark for several days, they unroll it, exterior side up, on the building platform. Then they

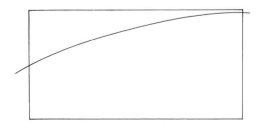

pull any loose bark off the sheet. The bark they are using for this 4-m (13-ft.) canoe is cut to 4.2 m (13¾ ft.). In forming the bow later on, a few centimeters will have to be trimmed from each end. Only 3 mm (⅛ in.) thick, this piece of bark is thinner than usual, and its narrow width of 85 cm (33½ in.) means that more

bark will have to be sewn on the sides than is ordinarily necessary.

All during the building process, boiling water is kept at the ready. They frequently pour it over the birch bark and cedar to make them more pliable.

Once the bark is spread out on the platform, a plywood frame is centered on top of it and weighted down with heavy stones. This frame, 76 cm (30 in.) wide and 3.65 m (12 ft.) long, is roughly the same size as the inwales and will be used to form the bottom of the canoe.

Other builders use the inside gunwales for this purpose and later raise the gunwales to their final position.

When the bark is well weighted down, William and Mary cut seven gores on each side of the bark, then turn the sides. These gores are about 50 cm (19½ in.) apart, correspond-

ing in position with the stakes in the building platform and with the middle gores at the central thwart. William and Mary always overlap the gores in the same direction, so that they are streamlined from the bow to the stern. It is this overlapping that gives their birchbark canoe a bow and a stern, although both ends of the canoe may look the same to the untrained eye. Other builders overlap from both ends to the middle, so that the gores are streamlined no matter which way the canoe is headed.

Should there already be a tear in the side of the bark sheet, this tear often will be used as a gore. The purpose of the gores is to give the canoe a proper shape. Without the gores, the canoe would be hogged—that is, the center of the canoe would be higher in relation to the two bows.

Some builders then sew the gores. William and Mary do not; their bark is held firmly between the inwale and the outwale. At this point, they raise and stake the sides of the canoe.

The preassembled inwale frame is tied at the ends and held apart by dummy thwarts. The dummy center thwart is 70 cm (27½ in.) long, the middle ones 58 cm (23 in.), and the small end ones 20 cm (8 in.).

For this canoe, the inwale measures 25 by 16 mm (1 by ⅝ in.) (on top) at the middle thwart and tapers to 16 by 13 mm (⅝ by ½ in.) (on top) at the inside of the bow where the two inwales are joined. William and Mary bevel the bottom edge of the inwale nearest the bark to receive the ribs later on, and they measure off the inwale in 50-mm (2-in.) intervals where the spruce root lashing and rib placements alternate. The top side of the outwale measures 32 by 13 mm (1¼ by ½ in.) and tapers to 19 by 10 mm (¾ by ⅜ in.) at the end.

Next they put the inner gunwale frame and the outwales in place, then insert hardwood stakes into their holes to hold up the sides of the canoe and to hold the gunwales in place. They place a piece of old sheathing inside the stakes to help support the bark. At this time, William and Mary work together to clamp the two bows temporarily. Even at this early forming of the bows, they try to keep them well aligned. Then they put stakes inside the canoe, planted against the frame on the bottom and

The plywood frame is weighted as it sits on the bark sheet. (Photo by David Gidmark.)

Mary Commanda cuts seven gores in each side of the bark sheet. These slits will be overlapped, rather than sewn. (Photo by David Gidmark, courtesy National Museum of the American Indian, Smithsonian Institution.)

Boiling water keeps the bark pliable as the bow is formed. (Photo by David Gidmark.)

The wedge under the bow increases the rocker. This is done at both ends. (Photo by David Gidmark, courtesy National Museum of the American Indian, Smithsonian Institution.)

Scrap bits of sheathing and stakes keep the bark in place after it is turned up. (Photo by David Gidmark, courtesy National Museum of the American Indian, Smithsonian Institution.)

The gunwales are clamped in place. (Photo by David Gidmark, courtesy National Museum of the American Indian, Smithsonian Institution.)

tied to the outside stakes. The assembly now has the approximate form of a canoe.

To form the rocker of the canoe, William slides a long wedge beneath each bow. He makes some adjustments with a measuring stick (*tipahigans*) to make sure that the gunwales are the proper height, both amidships and at the bows. Then he fastens them into place with temporary clamps. Next, he trims the bark almost even with the tops of the gunwales.

William is trying something a little different with this canoe: He is overlapping the bark on the inwale. Often when the ribs are placed in the canoe, they cause the inwale to ride up so that it is 13 mm (1/2 in.) or so higher than the outwale. Neither the *watap* lashing nor the wooden pegs in the gunwales seem to stop this riding up. With the bark overlapped over the inwale, this problem should be stemmed.

Before sewing the spruce root, a square hardwood peg is driven through the inwale and outwale at each lashing location. Later the lashing will hide the pegs.

Mary is in charge of sewing the gunwales. At each spot that must be bound, she makes four holes with a small awl (*mikos*) through the bark just below the gunwales. Then she passes a single length of spruce root around the gunwales eight times, twice through each hole. When each section is finished, the bark is sandwiched very tightly between the two cedar gunwales. It is more tightly bound than if nails had been used.

Spruce root stretches very slightly when wet so that it dries tight. It is an extremely useful material. The more time spent in the preparation of the spruce root, the better the finished job. Good builders not only make sure the root is strong, but also see to it that the spruce root is even and, particularly, that it is sewn evenly. Some of the finest builders of the past even varied the width of the spruce root lashing along the gunwale for decorative purposes. There are perhaps fifty or sixty intervals along the gunwales that require binding. This takes up much of the total time involved in making a canoe.

The next step is to cut mortises into the inwales with a chisel to receive the thwarts. When William puts the mortise into the inwale for the center thwart, the mortise goes only as deep as the bark, not through the bark. He is

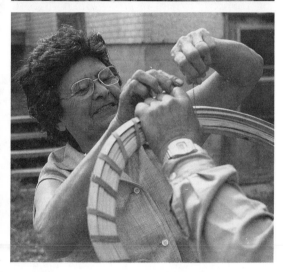

always careful to have the lashings on both sides of the mortise sites finished before cut-

ting the mortises, as the lashings will prevent a split in the inwale from spreading, should one occur.

The thwart then goes through the inwale only as far as the sandwiched bark and is lashed in place with spruce root. The paddler in an Indian canoe kneels in front of the thwart and leans back against it; therefore, a thwart, to support the weight, should be made of hardwood and not cedar.

William lashes the small thwarts near the bow, but only nails the center thwart in place temporarily. Then he removes the building frame from the canoe.

The ribs are formed by quartering the cedar log, then splitting away the heartwood. William splits the remaining piece in half with a froe, always starting at the small end of the log and going toward the butt end. Should a split begin to go off to one side, that side is kept as straight as possible while the thick side is bent away more sharply. He splits until he gets the rough form of the rib, roughly 10 mm (³/₈ in.) thick and 50 mm (2 in.) wide. In splitting cedar for ribs, great care is taken to split precisely, so that the two broad sides will not have to be carved later with the drawknife. In this way, the ribs are smooth and do not show the carving strokes. He then finishes the ribs with a drawknife on a carving horse. Shaped somewhat like a carpenter's horse, the carving horse has an arm in the center that holds the wood so that both hands can be used on the drawknife.

The ribs are notched to distinguish the butt end from the top end. Butt ends and top ends are alternated in order to distribute the tensile strength, which is stronger near the butt. Extra ribs are made in case any should be dam-

The excess bark must be trimmed above the gunwales. (Photo by David Gidmark, courtesy National Museum of the American Indian, Smithsonian Institution.)

Unlike the ribs, the stem-piece is split first at right angles to the grain, then in several sections with the grain. (Photo by David Gidmark, courtesy National Museum of the American Indian, Smithsonian Institution.)

With William's help, Mary ties the stem-piece with a basswood strip. (Photo by David Gidmark.)

Square wooden pegs are driven through the gunwale; they will later be concealed by lashing. (Photo by David Gidmark.)

The thwart will fit into the mortise that William is picking out. His chisel does not pierce the bark. (Photo by David Gidmark.)

The thwart is inserted, then tightly sewn. (Photo courtesy Viking Ship Museum, Roskilde, Denmark.)

Splitting the outwale makes it easier to bend the wood up toward the peak of the bow. (Photo by David Gidmark, courtesy National Museum of the American Indian, Smithsonian Institution.)

aged or broken in the building process. William makes a bundle of the ribs and soaks them in water several days before using them. This canoe will have thirty-six ribs.

The quality of the work in a birchbark canoe can be determined in a number of ways. One of the main ones is to examine the finish of the ribs. A builder who has taken great care in the making of the ribs has finished the surface so that it is almost perfectly smooth, something that might seem difficult with a crooked knife but is well within the reach of the mas-

ter builder. Other wooden parts should also be as smooth as possible. Pieces that show the splitting or have too many knife marks are the work of a less competent builder. Once one has seen a number of birchbark canoes, the skill of the really good builder is amazing.

The sheathing is more thinly split than the ribs but is two to three times as wide. These pieces are also soaked in water so that they will be easier to work with later.

Once the gunwales have been sewn to their entire length with spruce root, the Commandas begin the work of forming the bows.

The first step in forming the bow is to raise the ends of the inwales. William wets the inwales with hot water to make them easier to bend. The water is applied for a couple of feet near the bow where most of the bending is going to be done. He then raises the inwale bow from 12.5 cm (5 in.) off the tip of the building frame to 25 cm (10 in.) off the building frame. It is held in place with a support.

William fashions a triangular piece of cedar about 1 m (3 ft.) long to be the stem-piece. This he splits partially four times, leaving it unsplit at one end. The piece is split so that it will be easier to bend. He steams the piece for a few minutes, bends it to the bow curvature he wants, and ties it in that shape with a basswood strip to dry. The other stem-piece is bent the same way, care being taken to bend the second stem-piece to the same curvature as the first.

When the stem-pieces are dried in form, William and Mary fit them to the bows and clamp them temporarily in place. After the stem-piece is sewn in, the gunwale ends are bent slightly up and joined to it. The upper sweep of the gunwale ends is such that laminations have to be made to aid the bending. The gunwales are split three or four times back to the first lashing at the end thwart, or about

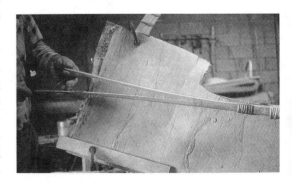

35 cm (14 in.) from the tip of the gunwale. When bending the gunwale ends upward, William and Mary apply hot water to them with a dipper.

Then, a little back from the bow, they add a cedar headboard (*otinimanganikadjigan*, or shoulder device) that is 30 cm (12 in.) high and 10 cm (4 in.) wide, with a thickness of 20 mm (³/₄ in.). This shoulders the two gunwales and is based on the bottom end of the stem-piece, giving added support.

William cuts the bark of the bow to the curvature he wants. Bow design is the chief distinguishing characteristic between the canoes of different tribes. The Ojibway had a bow that was greater than a semicircle, tumbling home toward the stern, whereas the Algonquin stem-piece generally pointed straight up. Some tribes had their own variations. A low bow might be employed if the canoeist wanted to go along streams with overhanging branches or to avoid taking too much wind on open lakes. Also, different builders within the same tribe had various ways of making a bow, although they generally stuck fairly close to their traditional pattern. One canoe maker could usually recognize another canoe maker's work.

After William has cut the bark of the bow, Mary's work begins again. She carefully stitches the cedar stem-piece to the bark with spruce root, creating a decorative bow. The bow is reinforced by lashing the two gunwales together just inboard of the stem-piece.

When the bows are finished, the canoe is nearing completion. The hull is shaped, the gunwales are in place and bound with spruce root, the ends are finished and cut a distinctive figure. Three operations remain: The ribs and sheathing have to be placed in, the gunwale covers have to be pegged to the gunwales, and the whole canoe has to be gummed.

Ideally, all the parts of the canoe should be prefinished. Before anything is joined together, the spruce root should be prepared and the ribs and sheathing split and laid out. Then when construction begins, the operation is not much more than a process of fitting things together.

William puts the final touches on the ribs, and Mary tapers the pieces of sheathing with a knife. They then submerge the ribs and sheathing in water again to make them less brittle and easier to use.

When it is time for the ribs to go into the canoe, William takes two at a time and places them abeam on the gunwales, then traces a line on the rib some distance inside the gunwale on each side of the canoe. William uses a piece of wood that is the width of three fingers to draw these lines. It is at these two points that the two ribs will be bent.

For insertion into the canoe, the ribs are

steamed, two at a time, for about five minutes. The old way of preparing the ribs is to soak them for several days, then to pour boiling water over them at the two points where they are to be bent. William has constructed a 2.5-m (8-ft.) long box of sheet metal, which is filled with water and heated electrically. This device allows him to steam ribs in five minutes with less bother.

The use of a steaming box, steel knife, awl, or carpenter's saw is not traditional, nor is felling a tree with a saw, for that matter. The builder can still end up with a traditional canoe, however, as these implements only serve to make the work easier and do not necessarily change the workmanship. By contrast, employing nails to fasten the inwale and

Temporarily bound back together with basswood, the split outwale is bent up. (Photo courtesy Viking Ship Museum, Roskilde, Denmark.)

Working as a team, William and Mary bend two steamed ribs at a time. (Photo by David Gidmark.)

The bent ribs are fitted into the canoe. (Photo by David Gidmark.)

Binders hold the ribs in position; the binders are held in place by cross braces. (Photo by David Gidmark.)

The ribs are removed when dry. Starting at the bow, Mary fits the sheathing in overlapping strips. (Photo by David Gidmark, courtesy National Museum of the American Indian, Smithsonian Institution.)

The bow is near completion. (Photo by David Gidmark.)

canoe. Two pieces about the dimensions of the gunwales are put in the bottom of the canoe, and then cross braces are wedged against them, forcing the ribs to stay in place. Under the thwarts, 15-cm (6-in.) sticks of wood are also wedged in to keep the binder toward the bottom of the canoe.

When dry, the ribs can be taken out and laid aside, while the sheathing is carefully placed, overlapping, to cover the entire inner hull right up to the gunwales. Once the sheathing is put in the bow, it is fitted past the headboard all the way to the stem-piece on the inside. In this way the sheathing gives extra protection for that section of bark between the headboard and the stem-piece.

William carves the rib ends to fit perfectly under the inner gunwale, then fits them back in

outwale together and hold down the gunwale cap or using pitch to seal the seams in the bark results in a birchbark canoe with significant nontraditional elements.

Ribs that William puts into this canoe are 57 mm (2¹/₄ in.) wide and 10 mm (³/₈ in.) thick. Their length varies according to their position in the canoe. After the ribs are steamed, he bends them with the knee in two places. He puts temporary sheathing into the canoe to duplicate the depth of the real sheathing, then fits the ribs into the canoe. When one rib is bent with another, the two ribs can be set amidships in the canoe, and the rib on top moved closer to the bow. The canoe narrows toward the bows, so the rib that had been inside the other one fits very well. After the set of two ribs is fitted into the canoe as snug against the bottom as it will go, it is left there. If it has a tendency to pop out, the set of ribs is clamped to the gunwale on each side. Frequently the builder breaks the final rib before the bow, to make it conform to the V shape of the bow profile.

After the ribs are fitted into the canoe, they are left there to dry. For this temporary fitting of the ribs, the builder puts a binder in the over the sheathing. He places the ribs in the canoe starting from the center thwart and going toward the bow. With the wooden mallet, he taps the rib neatly into place. The ribs are all tapped in at an angle at first, so that excess pressure is not exerted at any single spot. Going to the bow once or twice, he taps the ribs into an upright position as simultaneously as possible to distribute the pressure on the bark.

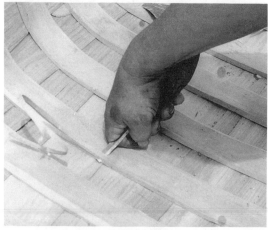

When this is done, William fits the gunwale cap (*apatapikáhigan*)—almost like a cedar gunwale turned on its side—over the two gunwales. This gunwale cover is a protection for the spruce root lashing. It is slightly hollowed on the bottom to receive the spruce root. He secures it in place using square hardwood pegs driven into the gunwales. The pegs are left overnight in the gunwale cap to allow for a little drying. The next day he pounds them in farther, if need be, and cuts them off. These caps may then be sanded or carved to create a smooth finish.

Now William must do a little finishing work on the canoe. This is sort of a polishing, wherein any mistakes are noted and corrected; it also includes a go-round of the canoe with the crooked knife. Square edges of ribs and gunwale caps are rounded slightly.

When a birchbark canoe is completed to this point, it is reasonably impervious to water. It is still necessary, however, to seal it completely with spruce gum.

Pieces of hard gum are gathered from wounds in spruce trees. This takes a great deal of gathering, because the builder might get very little from a single tree. Once he has a nice panful, William melts it down and then skims any impurities (dirt or flecks of wood) from the surface. At this point, fat and often powdered charcoal are added to the gum as tempering agents, the former so that the gum will be elastic enough not to crack, and the latter so that the mixture will not run in the heat of the sun. Then the gum is applied on the two ends, at all seams, and at any points along the

The deck-piece is fitted under the gunwale ends. (Photo by David Gidmark.)

Other builders bevel the edges of the ribs before fitting them into the canoe, but the Commandas do the smoothing afterward. (Photo by David Gidmark, courtesy National Museum of the American Indian, Smithsonian Institution.)

The gunwale cover protects the lashings of the gunwale. (Photo courtesy National Capital Commission.)

Square pegs are driven into the gunwale cover, then chiseled smooth. (Photo by David Gidmark.)

A design—in this case a bear—may be traced on the bark. (Photo by David Gidmark.)

The canoe is nearly ready to launch. (Photo by David Gidmark.)

Gumming the seams with spruce resin seals the canoe. The scalloped design under the gunwale is scraped, not a separate piece of bark. (Photo by David Gidmark.)

of the canoe, containing gum that had already been tempered. Because the gum had hardened in the pot, it could not fall out. If a leak developed in the canoe, the pot would be put over a little fire, the gum melted, and then a little applied to the spot on the canoe. The remainder then would harden again in the pot.

If the traveler had not brought a gum pot along, he could take a few hard knobs of spruce gum directly from the tree, chew them until they were soft, then apply the gum to the canoe.

When the gumming is complete, the canoe is finished. The canoe that William and Mary have constructed is 4.06 m (13 1/3 ft.) long, 83.8 cm (33 in.) in the beam, and 34.2 cm (13 1/2 in.) deep; it weighs 23.5 kg (52 lbs.).

William tries out the canoe by taking it to a lake for a trial run. He pays careful attention to the bottom of the canoe to see if there are any leaks. If he notices one, he takes the canoe up on shore, turns it over, and finds the leak by sucking air where he thinks it might be. When he finds the leak, which is probably in an area that has already been gummed, he lights a match or a small piece of birch bark to melt a little of the surrounding gum, and then uses it to seal the leak.

With proper care, there is no reason that the birchbark canoe cannot last as long as the person who owns it.

hull where it appears that there might be a small hole.

Sometimes it would happen that a canoe needed a little bit of extra gumming while in the woods. Often the canoeist carried a small tin gum pot hung by a small wire in the bow

V

James Jerome, Lac Barrière Algonquin, Rapid Lake, Québec

James Jerome is a member of the Lac Barrière Algonquin Band from Rapid Lake, Québec, about 300 km (180 mi.) north of Ottawa. He is one of only three skilled birchbark canoe builders remaining in this band of traditionally skilled builders and, at the same time, one of the handful of Indian birchbark canoe builders remaining in North America.

Born in 1918, Jim is a short man who walks slowly because of a slight limp in his right leg. Arthritis in both legs causes him great difficulty when walking in the woods.

Jim started helping his father build canoes when he was nine or ten; he had a pretty good ability by the time he was nineteen and first made a birchbark canoe when he was twenty-one. He has made about twenty birchbark canoes in his lifetime.

Many of his relatives were birchbark canoe makers. His father, when living on Lake Andostagan, about a day's paddle southwest of Lac Barrière, made fur trade canoes there with his brother and delivered the large birchbark canoes to the factor at the Hudson's Bay Company post at Lac Barrière. Jim recalls that the gunwales of the fur trade canoes were made of spruce, as were, occasionally, the gunwales of some of the smaller canoes. He remembers canoes as long as 5.5 m (18 ft.) being made.

In former times, according to Jim, roughly three-fourths of the men at Rapid Lake were capable of making birchbark canoes. This number seems to be very high compared with other reserves, and it is probably because as recently as a few decades ago canoes were the only transportation the Lac Barrière Indians had. To Jim's knowledge, no women were canoe makers in their own right.

Jim last used a birchbark canoe to any great extent in the 1940s. When he was a young boy, he would sometimes put a tarpaulin up in a birchbark canoe to use as a sail. He remembers going as a ten-year-old with his parents and others in two birchbark canoes to Maniwaki, more than 150 km (90 mi.) south by water, to get supplies.

Jim's wife, Angèle, participated in canoe making only to the extent of preparing some spruce root and sewing it along the gunwales.

The author observed Jim building a birchbark canoe in 1989. Two French film-

Jim Jerome shows Corey how to select a cedar tree. The straightness of grain, revealed when a bark strip is removed, will determine whether the wood can be split into ribs. (Photo by David Gidmark.)

The felled cedar is split first in half, then in quarters. (Photo by David Gidmark.)

Jim uses a crooked knife to carve the ribs. (Photo by David Gidmark.)

makers were along to record the entire process on video.

Jim and Angèle would build the canoe at their summer camp about 2 km (1¹/₂ mi.) across the lake, on a point of land about 75 m (250 ft.) long. Jim and Angèle had a tent there, as well as a canoe-building bed and a pit for making an open fire.

Before our arrival, Jim had cut long cedar for gunwales and had carved two. He had not yet found cedar for ribs or sheathing nor brought any spruce root into the camp. He and his son, Corey, now set out to find cedar for ribs and sheathing. They took their boat into a bay about a kilometer from the point, and Jim began scanning the shoreline for cedar. When he spotted a likely place, Jim and Corey would pull the boat up to shore. Jim was looking for a tree from which he could get a 1.5-m (5-ft.) log for ribs and sheathing. He preferred that it be knot-free, though he said that he was ready to take a log that was clear on one side even if there were knots on the other. But he insisted that the grain of the tree be straight. Good builders always sought very straight, long cedar for the gunwales, especially for the inwales, but many were not so particular with the cedar for the ribs, feeling that as the ribs had to be bent anyway in forming the canoe, a curve in the wood was not a problem.

If a tree was close to being good, Jim made an ax cut near the bottom and pulled the end of the bark, taking off a strip up the trunk.

When the strip indicated a straight grain, he would have the cedar he needed.

There were big cedars in the woods—many more than 40 cm (15³/₄ in.) in diameter and with fairly straight grain. Often we would come upon a cedar that some Indian had felled. These were evidently the good ones. We could see from the way that short cedar blocks had been split that they had been looking for *tikinâgan* (cradleboard) backs. A piece of cedar about 4 cm (1¹/₂ in.) thick, 40 cm (15³/₄ in.) wide, and 75 cm (29¹/₂ in.) long is fashioned to give a nice, even board that becomes a *tikinâgan* back. Pieces that were close but not quite acceptable were here and there where trees had been cut.

After a couple of hours, Jim found an acceptable cedar. He gave Corey the chain saw, and Corey took down the tree and cut two 1.5-m (5-ft.) logs. Jim used two axes to split the log, first into halves and then quarters. He then had Corey take the bark off the quarter logs.

Jim was extremely concerned about the birch bark, which has been getting increasingly

harder to find. Looking for bark for this canoe was the longest, most arduous search I have ever made for birch bark, and I now think that bark in the Rapid Lake area (generally about 150 km [90 mi.] north of Maniwaki) is, for some reason, drier than bark farther south.

Jim said that good birch bark would be found high on a hill with hardwoods such as maple and yellow birch. He felt that birch that grew in low areas would be of poor quality. He said that bark was sometimes thinner at the bottom of the trunk than at the top. Ideally, the eyes should be short and widely spaced, and, according to him, dark eyes meant unhealthy bark and light eyes meant healthy bark.

The search for bark took several days. In all we covered nearly 1,000 km (600 mi.) in several trips. For the first three trips, Jim came with us. But as he had arthritic legs and had trouble walking, Corey and I eventually left him at the point to work on ribs and gunwales, and we set out alone. We finally found a tree that yielded a sheet of suitable bark about 1.15 m (45 in.) wide and 3 mm (⅛ in.) thick.

For thwarts, Jim favored yellow birch, though he said that any hardwood would do. He cut a short log, split it into quarters, and then took it down with the ax to close to the thwart size, from which point he finished it with a crooked knife. Then he hung it vertically so that it would dry for a day or two while he was doing other work. If it twisted slightly during this time, he would take the twist out with the crooked knife.

Often, in finishing some of the wood like ribs, sheathing, and thwarts, Jim would use a small hand plane instead of the crooked knife. He did this more often on the sheathing than on any other members. Most of the finishing work with the ribs, gunwales, and thwarts was done with the crooked knife.

It was important to finish the gunwale batten well, because from this batten would be split two equal gunwales.

Jim started the split with a knife, then worked it wider with his hands, always careful that he did not go too fast and lose the split off to one side. He kept the split very carefully in the middle of the batten. As the split lengthened, he used the leg of his table for leverage to help in keeping the split centered.

Once the gunwales were split, Jim carved

Before felling a birch tree, the men place logs where the butt will land so that the trunk of the tree, with its precious bark, will not crash on the ground and be damaged. (Photo by David Gidmark.)

The removal of the bark starts with a cut down the length of the trunk. (Photo by David Gidmark.)

The sheet comes off smoothly if the bark is not dry. (Photo by David Gidmark.)

Jim's crooked knife has a moose antler handle and a blade that started out as a commercially produced hoof knife. (Photo by David Gidmark.)

The thwarts are made from yellow birch. Jim hangs them to dry. (Photo by David Gidmark.)

The gunwales are split from a single batten of cedar. Jim works slowly, using a table leg (the upright on the left) as a lever. (Photo by David Gidmark.)

Angèle Jerome returns to camp with a large roll of white spruce root for the lashings. (Photo by David Gidmark.)

helped in getting materials, he did not participate much in the actual work on the canoe.

Angèle harvested the white spruce root up on a little rise behind the point. She dug at the ground with the back of an ax until she found a root, then she pulled the root out toward its end. When roots crossed each other, as they frequently did, she fed one under the other. Once she had gathered enough roots, she rolled them up and returned to camp, where she put the roll in the lake and weighted it down with rocks.

Angèle had to work at her job in the dispensary during the weekdays, which made it a bit difficult for Jim. This was particularly evident when the spruce root had to be split. To help split the root, he hired Lina Nottaway, a respected craftswoman in her seventies who lived nearby.

Jim chained a large barrel over the fire to boil the root. Lina first split the root in half, then split out the middle half of each section and discarded it. She would start the split with a knife, widen it with her fingers, then hold one root end in her mouth and the other in one hand, and use the other hand to hold the intact root at the split and to help guide the split. The outer part of the root still had the bark on. She put this in the water to boil so that the bark was easier to remove.

To make the ribs, Jim took a batten about 1.5 m (5 ft.) long and started a split with his

them a little more with the crooked knife. Then he put them high in the branches of a tree so that someone would not step on them and break them. A few days before using them to make the building frame that would then go in the canoe, he would put them in the water to soak.

The family was very much part of the canoe-building operation, but though Corey had

a little leverage to work the blank, he used a fork in a tree. If the wood was cut green, Jim did not soak the pieces of sheathing before using them.

Lina Nottaway splits a length of spruce root. (Photo by David Gidmark.)

More cedar battens are split, this time for sheathing. The fork in the tree provides leverage. (Photo by David Gidmark.)

ax. As soon as the split was wide enough to get his fingers in it, he worked the split the rest of the way along the batten using his knees or whatever other point of leverage happened to be handy.

Logs for the ribs were always split perpendicular to the bark until they were in quarters or eighths. From that point on, splits were parallel to the bark.

Jim did not use sapwood (the outer portion of the wood) for the ribs, because it was hard to work with the crooked knife. The ribs were to be bent toward the sapwood, rather than toward the heart of the log. Most of the time he used the crooked knife to finish the ribs, but occasionally he used the hand plane. As ribs in Algonquin canoes go, Jim's were fairly large, about 6 cm (2³⁄₈ in.) wide and 10 mm (³⁄₈ in.) thick in the area of the center thwart. They tapered minimally toward the bow.

The sheathing was made somewhat in the manner of the ribs, only the pieces were split thinner. He began the initial splitting with a birch mallet and two birch wedges, and sometimes used an ax. When the blanks were about 2.5 cm (1 in.) thick, he did the fine splitting with a strong-bladed knife. Sitting on a bench, he started the split with the knife, then continued it by hand. If the split started to run in one direction, he would apply pressure in the opposite direction to bring the split back. He worked the split along with his hands all the way to the end of the blank. When he needed

The building bed was located under some small birches that provided shade. When Jim was close to beginning construction, he leveled the bed as best he could.

The bark had been soaking in the lake, tied to a little makeshift dock. When Jim was ready to start, Corey took the roll from the water, and they unrolled it, white side up, on the

Jim looks for short, widely spaced, light-colored eyes. The sheet of bark must also be large enough for his building frame. (Photo by David Gidmark.)

Excess bark is shaved from the sheet. (Photo by David Gidmark.)

The building bed must be level, so the builders smooth it under the bark before proceeding. (Photo by David Gidmark.)

Even though the bark has been soaked in the lake, hot water must be poured over it to make the material supple enough to be worked. (Photo by David Gidmark.)

The bow can now be folded and raised. (Photo by David Gidmark.)

building bed. Then they took knives, with which they pulled excess bark from the sheet and tried to cut away imperfections.

The building frame was 3.55 m (12 ft. 2 in.) long and 73.66 cm (29 in.) wide. They placed it on the bark, centered at first by eye. Then Jim took one of the gunwales, about 4.25 m (14 ft.) long, and used this to draw a line that ran along the center of the bark, fore to aft, but was drawn only from the tip of the frame to the edge of the bark at each bow. The tip of the frame was the same number of inches from each side of the bark sheet.

When the frame was centered, it was time to cut the gores. Jim cut seven gores on each side of the canoe. He had a 40-cm-long (15³/₄-in.-long) measure that he used for spacing the gores. As the gores approached the bow, he slanted them slightly toward the bow, so that once the sides were put up and the sheet was overlapped at each gore, the gores would be as nearly vertical as possible in the finished canoe.

He next applied hot water to the bark sheet, particularly at each bow where it had to be folded sharply. To help create the canoe's rocker, he put a cedar block a bit over 6 cm (2³/₈ in.) high under the tip of the building frame to prop it up. And when the bow bark was folded, he used a split cedar batten to clamp the bow bark in a folded position.

To put up the sides of the canoe, he used birch pickets about 7 cm (2³/₄ in.) in diameter. He put one fairing piece about 4.25 m (14 ft.) long inboard of the stakes on each side and against the bark next to the ground, and another on each side at approximately gunwale height.

The beam of the main sheet was not wide enough, so Jim cut two pieces of bark, which

A fairing strip keeps the sides of the canoe smooth when the outside stakes are pounded in. (Photo by David Gidmark.)

about one-third down from the top of the inwale. To make the mortise, he first traced the end of the thwart and then made the hole with a chisel and knife.

Then Jim put the inwale assembly into the canoe. To set the height of the inwale assembly off the bark, he had a measure that fixed the distance from the underside of the center thwart to the top of the crosspiece on the building frame at that point at 20.32 cm (8 in.). The distance from the underside of the intermediate thwart to the top of the crosspiece on the frame at that point was 22.86 cm (9

Using a measuring stick, Jim marks off the locations of the lashing and ribs along the gunwale. (Photo by David Gidmark.)

he put along the sides to widen the main sheet. These were sewn in place later.

Jim then finished the inwale frame. He did the final finishing of the inwales by holding both in one hand as he worked with the crooked knife. That way, he would compare one against the other as he went along. The inwales were cut to 4.25 m (14 ft.) and measured 3.8 by 1.9 cm (1½ by ¾ in.) at the center thwart, tapering to 2.2 by 1.6 cm (⅞ by ⁵⁄₆ in.) toward the ends.

Jim measured 5-cm (2-in.) intervals along the inwales; these were to be alternate lashing and rib locations. Because thwarts are lashed to the gunwales, each thwart end constitutes a lashing spot. There were six lashings between the center and intermediate thwarts, and six lashings between the intermediate and the end thwarts. Jim then put the inwales into his steaming tube in order to steam the ends. When they were ready, he removed them from the tube and placed the inwales one after another on a flat surface. In order to form a curve, he pulled up the end of each inwale with his hands while stepping on it at several places just short of the end. He then beveled the lower inboard edge of the inwale to receive the rib ends later.

Jim next mortised the thwart ends into the inwale. For the center thwart, the mortise was

For steaming the inwales, Jim uses a length of drain pipe stopped with a can at the lower end. This end is lowered into a fire to keep the water hot. (Photo by David Gidmark.)

After their steam bath, the inwales are bent up. (Photo by David Gidmark.)

in.). He used wooden clamps to fix the inwale and outwale in place.

To raise the inwale frame, Jim put a temporary headboard under each end. The shoulders of the headboard were 38.10 cm (15 in.) high.

He drew a guideline outboard on the bark

for sewing the side panel to the main sheet. The side panel was about 1.8 m (5 ft. 11 in.)

A side panel of bark extends the narrow sheet with which Jim has to work. (Photo by David Gidmark.)

Jim cuts the mortises for the thwarts before the gunwale is lashed in place. (Photo by David Gidmark.)

A dry run: the fit of thwarts, gunwales, and side panels is checked and adjusted. (Photo by David Gidmark.)

After using an awl to pierce the bark, Jim threads spruce root through the main sheet and side panel. (Photo by David Gidmark.)

long and 3 mm (1/8 in.) thick, slightly thicker than the main sheet of bark, which averaged about 2.25 mm (1/10 in.). The stitch used for sewing the side panel was a double-thong stitch. Jim lamented that the main bark sheet was not wide enough to avoid using a side panel. He said that this made for much extra work.

After the side panels were sewn to the main sheet, he checked the height of the inwales and outwales and then clamped them again.

Jim next cut the bark down to the gunwales. Bark was not folded over the inwale. He said that the bark would be folded over the inwale (generally to keep the inwale from riding up from the intense rib pressure later) only if the builder planned to nail the gunwales instead of lashing them with spruce root. He said that Indians today generally nailed the gunwales if they made canoes for themselves.

Jim nailed the inwale and the outwale together; these nails would all be covered later by the spruce root lashing. They were put at every lashing near the thwarts and every other lashing between the thwarts. The nails were pounded from inboard to outboard against an ax head so that the tips of the nails would be curled.

Angèle and my wife, Ernestine, lashed the gunwales. They punched holes under the gunwale with a triangular awl. For each location, they took a length of prepared white spruce root about 2 m (6 ft.) long. They put the root through each hole two or three times and lashed the inwale and outwale together, the bark sandwiched in between, until the spot marked earlier for the lashing had been completely filled.

While the women were lashing the gunwales, Jim made his stem-pieces. First he split out a couple of lengths of cedar about 70 cm (27 1/2 in.) long. Unlike the ribs and sheathing, these were split perpendicular to the bark. He carved a tapered piece with his crooked knife. The stem-piece was 45 mm (1 3/4 in.) wide and tapered from a thickness of 16 mm (5/8 in.) to 10 mm (3/8 in.). The thinner edge would be outboard when the stem-piece was bent.

He wrapped some cord about midway down the length of the stem-piece. This was to stop the splits in the stem-piece batten. He made several splits down to the cord, then soaked the split end in boiling water. Once it

and the lashing changed to a cross-stitch that crossed over itself at the cutwater. At this point, he cut off the top of the stem and the ends of the outwales.

In a canoe that Jim had made in 1985, he had put a serrated reinforcing bark the entire length of the canoe under the outwale, but this newer canoe had no reinforcing bark.

Once he had entirely lashed the gunwales and had lashed the thwarts into their mortises, he prepared to bend the ribs.

Jim suspended the canoe slightly off the ground by tying the end thwarts to the cross-pieces on the stakes near the bow. This is done so that the weight of the canoe does not pop the ribs out when they are inserted in the canoe to dry.

The ribs had been soaking in the water for a few days. (Sometimes, if the wood was green, he did not soak the ribs very long—maybe only two hours.) Before steaming the ribs, Jim first put some temporary sheathing in the bottom of the canoe. His fire was about 3 m (10 ft.) from the canoe. The rib steamer was an old drainpipe that he had closed with a tin can at the bottom end. This he filled with water. He stuck the closed end of the pipe in the fire; the other end of the pipe was wired to a post he had planted in the ground.

Before steaming the ribs, he placed them across the gunwales and marked them off about three finger lengths in from the gunwale. To bend the ribs, he first placed a pair in the steaming tube and left them in for about five minutes. Then he removed the ribs, sat down on a block of firewood, and bent them over

The excess bark is trimmed. Jim cuts it flush with the gunwales instead of folding it over. (Photo by David Gidmark.)

A wooden clamp squeezes the bark between the inwale and outwale. (Photo by David Gidmark.)

For the stem-pieces, lengths of cedar are split perpendicular to the bark, then steamed and bent. (Photo by David Gidmark.)

had soaked for about four minutes, he sat and bent the stem-piece at his knee. When it was bent to the proper curvature, he tied it with a cord to hold its shape and hung it in a tree to dry.

When the stem-pieces were dry, he fit them into the bows of the canoe. The top of the stem was fitted in between the ends of the inwales and nailed there. The bark was then trimmed to the bow profile. The ends of the bark did not meet beyond the stem, but only came to the sides of the outboard edge of the stem. Then the bow was lashed with a double-thong stitch started from the heel of the stem,

(Left) A stem-piece is fitted into the bow. (Photo by David Gidmark.)

(Right) The ends of the outwales are cut after the stem-pieces are in place. (Photo by David Gidmark.)

(Left) The bark is trimmed to match the bow profile. (Photo by David Gidmark.)

(Right) Working on a different canoe, Jim lashes the bow. Note the serrated reinforcing bark piece, which extends the length of the outwale. The canoe pictured in most of the photos in this chapter has no such reinforcing strip. (Photo by David Gidmark.)

The frame, which shows the dimensions of the bottom of the canoe, is lined up on top of the gunwales and the ribs are laid across, in position. Jim marks where the ribs will be bent. (Photo by David Gidmark.)

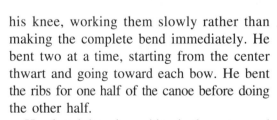

his knee, working them slowly rather than making the complete bend immediately. He bent two at a time, starting from the center thwart and going toward each bow. He bent the ribs for one half of the canoe before doing the other half.

He placed them in position in the canoe and pushed the pair snugly against the bottom, leaving the two ribs together. When all the ribs were bent and in the canoe, he removed the top rib of each pair and put it one place forward of its mate. All the ribs remained in place, perhaps thanks to his earlier having raised the canoe a few centimeters off the ground.

Next, Jim put the binder in the canoe. These two gunwale-like pieces of cedar were approximately 4 m (13 ft.) long, or long enough to press against all the ribs. They were also approximately 5 cm (2 in.) wide. He first spread them with a cross brace under each thwart, then added braces until there were ten forcing the binder against the ribs. To force the binder down against the bottom, he forced little 10-cm-long (4-in.-long) braces under the center thwart and the two intermediate thwarts. He placed no braces to force the binder down from the two end thwarts. He did all measuring for the horizontal and vertical braces by eye.

After the binder was in place, Jim continued to adjust the ribs so that they would be perfectly vertical and placed snugly against the bottom of the canoe. To do this, he would tap the rib a little sideways along the bottom or use his hammer to tap the end of the rib down.

When he was satisfied with the placement of the ribs and binder, he nailed several cross-pieces across the top of the gunwales to keep the gunwales from spreading under pressure from the ribs while drying.

Jim put the canoe in the sun so that the ribs would dry whenever the sun shone. Then he did some work on the sheathing.

After he had split blanks that were about 3 cm (1¼ in.) thick, he used a strong-bladed knife to begin the splits, then continued them by hand all the way to the end of each blank. When he needed a little leverage to work the blank, he used a fork in a tree.

Jim said that he needed about thirty of these pieces for his canoe. He used the pieces whole for the middle of the canoe, and cut those for each bow a little shorter. Jim said that he did not soak the sheathing before using it, as the wood was green.

Jim put a tin of tar on the fire to soften up. He applied the tar with a wooden spatula to the sewing of the side panels. Then he put over the tarred holes a 5-cm-wide (2-in.-wide) strip of canvas that he had cut from a larger piece. No tar was applied over the canvas. Jim said that tar was easier to work with than spruce gum, as it stayed soft longer. He had often used gum from white and black spruce.

Tar was applied on the inside of the hull under the two added side pieces so that the side pieces would stick to the main bark sheet. Tar

The curve of the ribs is extreme at the bow. Jim bends them two at a time. When the bottom rib of this pair is seated, the top rib will be slid forward toward the bow. (Photo by David Gidmark.)

Braces hold the binders in place while the ribs dry. Jim suspends the canoe—it hangs from ropes passing under the end thwarts—so that the ribs will not be affected by the weight of the canoe as they dry. (Photo by David Gidmark.)

For additional stability, braces are nailed across the gunwales. The serrated reinforcing strip of bark identifies this as a different canoe. (Photo by David Gidmark.)

was also applied inside on each side of the stem-piece.

To help in placing the sheathing in the canoe, Jim fashioned some makeshift ribs of

When the ribs are dry, they are removed so that the bark can be made watertight. Angèle gums the inboard seam with roofing tar and then covers it with a strip of canvas. (Photo by David Gidmark.)

sapwood from the cedar he had just been using. He beveled the ends of each and inserted one at the rib location just outboard of the intermediate thwart. The purpose of this support was to hold the sheathing in place while he fitted the real ribs. He placed another in the rib position next to the center thwart; this was to hold the middle set of sheathing.

The first pieces of sheathing were fitted toward the bow. He cut off the end of a piece of sheathing so that it would fit snugly into the crack where the bark met the stem-piece. After these were in place, he worked on the middle set of sheathing, putting each piece under the makeshift rib as he went along. Each new piece of sheathing overlapped the one below it. The tar gave Jim a bit of trouble; the pieces of sheathing stuck to it when he didn't

A temporary rib holds the sheathing in place as Jim overlaps their edges. (Photo by David Gidmark.)

want them to. It got on his hands and further hindered his work, and it also stained some of the cedar. He said he would later use some gasoline to remove the tar from his hands and from the cedar.

Jim started placing the ribs in the canoe for

their final insertion. He started at the bow, where all the sheathing had already been placed.

The first rib he inserted was the one inboard the end thwart. He omitted the rib outboard of the same thwart; this he would put in later. He had earlier penciled the outboard side of the ribs even with the gunwales. Now, with his crooked knife, he beveled the ends of the first rib and inserted it on the outboard side of the lower inwale in the bevel that had been made there.

He left the rib slightly short of vertical, waiting until later to drive it home, when he would also be using hot water to help the bark adjust. Now he did not use hot water.

He continued inserting the ribs on one half of the canoe all the way to the center thwart. The ribs were all short of the vertical, and the rib next to the center thwart was left out, as there would not be room to insert the two center ribs while the rest of the ribs were not in their vertical position. When he finished one end, he inserted the ribs in the canoe on the other end.

When all the ribs were partially driven home, he took the big bucket of hot water from the fire and poured it inside the canoe. He tipped the canoe from side to side, sloshing the hot water around so that it would wet the sheathing and bark beneath it. He let the canoe sit for half an hour, then began hitting the ribs home to the vertical.

To hit the ribs in partially, Jim had used a steel-headed hammer. But now, because the hammer might mark the soft cedar, he used a wooden mallet to hit the ribs to the vertical. Then he switched to the hammer again, this time placing a long piece of cedar against the rib and hitting that, rather than hitting the ribs directly.

The rib ends went in quite tightly. Any rib ends that had not been cut short enough he trimmed about 1 cm at a time with his crooked knife. If any were too short—he had misjudged a couple of times—he slipped a piece of folded bark over the ends of the rib to take up the slack.

When he had all the ribs in between both end thwarts, he put the first bow rib in. In the canoe he had made in 1985, the rib had gone in with such pressure that the bark had split.

The split, about 7 cm (2³/₄ in.) long and 1 cm (³/₈ in.) wide, was in the bottom of the canoe directly aft of the base of the stem-piece.

To make the deck-piece on each bow, Jim took a piece of summer bark, tried to flatten it, measured it against the outside of the outwale, and cut it. He nailed it flat with two nails in the outwale on each side. There was a little overhang on each deck-piece, which he trimmed off with the crooked knife.

Jim steamed the gunwale caps in his steaming tube before he nailed them on the canoe. He measured one cap at a time, making sure that it was long enough for the canoe. Then he found the midpoint of the gunwale cap, marked it, and centered it in the middle of the

lashing at the end of the center thwart. He nailed the gunwale cap all along every 20 cm (8 in.) or so. Once in a while, he drove the nail into the spruce root lashing; this did not seem to cause Jim any regret, although he generally tried to avoid it. The caps came to a point at the tip of the bow and at the end of the deck-piece.

Jim had originally made pencil lines for the sewing that would secure the side panels to the main bark sheet. Now he trimmed the bark above the sewing to within 2 cm (³/₄ in.) of the stitches. This was so that the roughly 4-cm-wide (1¹/₂-in.-wide) tar strip would cover both the sewing and the top of the main bark sheet. To do this, he used a sharp kitchen knife. So that he wouldn't cut through the added bark panel, he pushed a flat cedar stick between the two pieces of bark and under where he was cutting the outer piece with a knife.

Jim collected nodules of spruce sap from several trees in the woods. He melted this sap, and then poured the mixture into a piece of potato sack with a stick on each end. With the sticks, he twisted the pouch so that the purified spruce gum was extruded into a pan. To this he added grease as a tempering agent.

He applied the gum to the sewing of the side panel, making sure he covered the spruce

With a wooden mallet he taps the ribs into place. He lets the ribs rest and adjust for several hours before bringing them to vertical. (Photo by David Gidmark.)

Gunwale caps are ready for the canoe with the serrated reinforcing bark. (Photo by David Gidmark.)

root, the root holes, and the spot where the main bark ended. This gave a strip of gum that averaged 4 cm (1½ in.) wide. Then he applied the gum with his spatula over all the spruce root, the holes through which the root was laced, and particularly all along the outside of the stem-piece where it was sandwiched between the ends of the bark, beginning inboard about 5 cm (2 in.) of where the bow lashing started at the bottom of the stem-piece.

Then he sealed the bows by pressing two strips of canvas, each about 5 cm (2 in.) wide and 40 cm (15¾ in.) long, over the gum. When it was properly stuck to the gum, he applied gum over it. This second gumming hid the canvas, for the most part, and made a neat job of the bow. After he finished with the first bow, he did the second in the same fashion, and the canoe was completed.

Jim later sold this birchbark canoe for $2,200 to a private individual from Ontario.

The finshed canoe is ready for the lake. (Photo by David Gidmark.)

VI

Daniel Sarazin, Golden Lake Algonquin, Golden Lake, Ontario

The following chapter was recorded by Denis Alsford in 1970.

Daniel Sarazin was born in 1901 on Golden Lake Reserve. He started making canoes in 1924 and made about ten before giving it up three years later. Over the next twenty-eight years, he made only model canoes as a hobby. Then, in 1956, he was asked to go to Toronto to make a full-size canoe in public at the Toronto Exhibition. From then until 1969, he returned to Toronto each year to build a canoe, and made about sixty canoes altogether during that time.

He also is a student of canoe building, trying constantly to improve and to improvise when he is not able to get traditional materials, and frequently referring to books on the subject.

Dan works as a carpenter on the reserve. As we drove around together looking for materials for the canoe he was building, he obviously knew the district well and was able to recognize instantly a tree that was in the right soil and was of the right size and suitability for the work he was doing. And this at thirty miles per hour!

Daniel Sarazin, 1970. (Photo by Denis Alsford, National Museums of Canada.)

Dan built most commonly *wâbanäki tcîmân* type canoes, with or without a headboard, but would upon request build the old-style Algonquin canoe. When the author first visited Dan on June 29, 1970, he had one of this type hanging in his workshop waiting to be picked up. He had decorated it with a strip of birch bark sewn directly beneath the gunwale. He had also inserted two thwarts about 30 cm

(12 in.) apart, which he had joined by lashings that formed a netting pattern to create a seat, an idea the author suspects he obtained from one of his books.

In 1970 I watched Dan Sarazin complete a canoe that he had started two weeks before (now in the National Museum of Man) and returned to collect birch bark and see the beginnings of two other canoes in order to observe the entire process. Although I observed the work out of sequence, it is presented here in the correct order, and Dan read the manuscript to comment, correct, and add where he felt it necessary.

Traditionally, canoe making would take place outside on the ground and be subject to the vagaries of the weather, but Dan was fortunate enough to own an old Indian house on the reserve (built originally by him for another family) across the road from his own house, and this he used as a workshop. At the time of my visit it had no electricity, but this just meant shorter hours in the winter, and he hoped to be able to rectify the situation in the future. Thus he was able to continue his work in all weather, he had no fear that his tools would be lost or borrowed, the insect problem was lessened, he had a stove that supplied him with heat in winter, and most of the worries that would normally be his were reduced to a minimum.

Although his aim was always to produce the authentic article, he did not consider the methods he employed to be of great importance. He was always prepared to adopt a new method if it added to the ease of building. To this end he used a building bed of planks with predrilled holes for the stakes, and to eliminate the continual bending and stretching that would normally be part of the task, he had raised this onto a pair of sawhorses.

Birch bark for canoes is becoming more and more difficult to find in the Golden Lake region; the reservation no longer has any large trees that are suitable, and off the reservation all the land is owned by the state, the province, or privately, and most of the larger trees have been cut from those sources as well. Dan has to rely on local landowners who are willing to help when they have a suitable tree, or else get the bark from the local mill, which charges $20 or more for a piece. Occasionally a fallen tree will yield a usable piece. When Dan does collect his own bark, he gets it after felling the tree. But he insisted that in the old days it would have been taken while the tree still stood, and he took the bark from a live tree to demonstrate how it was done.

Dan, his son Kevin, and I had set out to collect some cedar for the gunwales and ribs that Dan had cut down about six weeks previously, but en route we also looked for a suitable birch tree. We stopped at the roadside by a heavily wooded area just north of Lake Doré. Dan had been here before and wanted to check some trees he had seen two years earlier. We went into the woods, and with his ax he took samples from three birch trees. From each he cut out a small piece about 6 by 4 cm (2³⁄₈ by 1¹⁄₂ in.) at shoulder height. The first tree was 1.44 m (4 ft. 9 in.) in circumference at the point where the bark had been removed, the second 1.65 m (5 ft. 5 in.), and the third 1.62 m (5 ft. 4 in.). The first two were too thin, but the third one Dan declared satisfactory. Several other trees showed signs of Dan's earlier visits.

In selecting a tree, Dan took into consideration not only its size but also its accessibility in terms of what was around the base of the tree. Would he be able to get a ladder down safely? Was there room for him to lay the bark out when it came off, or would it get snagged on a bush or another tree?

To be suitable, a tree had to be straight and free of branches for the first 6 m (20 ft.); otherwise the bark would be difficult to get off and would have a hole in it. The higher up the tree, the better the quality of the bark. The preferred time to take the bark is midsummer, but it was late August when we went. Dan said that in late summer the bark adheres tighter to the tree, and as he worked he suggested that it would have been better if this particular bark had been taken at least a week earlier.

The day before we went, Dan had made a ladder from odd lengths of timber he had in his workshop, and we took along some extra pieces in order to lengthen the ladder if necessary. In the old days, Dan related, the Indians would have made a ladder from branches cut on the spot and tied together, then discarded when the job was done. We also took with us an ax, a jackknife, a claw hammer, nails, and some pieces of string.

Once Dan had selected his tree, we cleared

an area around the tree about 3 m (10 ft.) in radius, assembled the ladder to reach the greatest height possible, and leaned it up against the tree. Dan climbed the ladder and, using the jackknife, cut a strip around the tree about 40 mm (1½ in.) wide and as high as he could reach, about 4 m (13 ft.) from the ground. Then, from the top down, he made a cut as straight as possible, and eased the left-hand side off carefully for about 40 mm (1½ in.). He slowly continued cutting and easing off the bark down the tree until about 90 cm (3 ft.) from the base. Then he cut another strip around the tree below the first, this time 20 cm (8 in.) wide, and peeled it off. Dan was aided by his son Kevin. They frequently had to alter the length of the ladder depending on the height at which they were working.

Once the first couple of centimeters (about 1 in.) had been peeled off with the jackknife, Dan then went to another birch tree and cut off a piece of bark about 25 cm (10 in.) square. He quickly cut this into a disc shape and trimmed the edge to a point. This he then used as a circular knife, rolling it round and round between the bark and the trunk, pressing it into the joint and easing the bark off slowly up and down its length. After he had thus peeled off about 60 cm (2 ft.) of the bark, he started the other side in the same manner, and slowly the bark was loosened. When only about 30 cm (1 ft.) of the bark remained in place, splits began to appear laterally, and to stop them from getting any worse, Dan quickly found a basswood tree and made some binding from the bark. He drilled two holes through the birch bark about 2.5 cm (1 in.) apart on either side of the split and tied the basswood binding through, thus stopping the splits from lengthening.

He then cut a straight basswood pole about 3.6 m (12 ft.) long and 5 cm (2 in.) in diameter and jammed it between the bark and the trunk to serve as a long wedge. Dan pushed from the bottom and Kevin, up the ladder, from the top, until eventually the bark fell off. Fortunately it remained intact. Just before the bark came off, Kevin tied string around the top so that the bark would slide down the tree and then gradually work away from the bottom of the tree, but the string broke just as the bark came loose.

The bark was not the best, and at one stage a spot was discovered where a branch had broken off earlier; this spot had not been noticed during Dan's examination of the tree, and it caused some difficulties in removal and was responsible for one of the tears.

The entire operation had taken two hours and fifty minutes. Once the bark was down,

Dan cuts a small piece of birch bark into a circle, sharpens the edge all around, and rolls it up and down the trunk, thereby prying the bark from the tree. (Photo by Denis Alsford, National Museums of Canada.)

we laid it out flat with the outside uppermost, rolled it up, tied it with string, and then carried it out of the woods to the car.

Dan uses cedar for the ribs, gunwales, and lining, but as with birch, there are very few trees in his area these days of suitable size. For the lining material, the tree needs to be about 60 cm (2 ft.) or more in diameter and, like the birch, is not to be found easily. The lining is made from the inner centimeter or so immediately beneath the bark; this portion of the tree is softer and easier to work than the harder center section. Here again, Dan often has to rely on the local mill for a supply.

In selecting a cedar, Dan looks for a straight-grained tree preferably no less than 50 cm (20 in.) in diameter. A smaller one, at least 30 cm (1 ft.), will do for gunwales and ribs but not for the lining. A straight-grained cedar can be determined by looking at the bark; if the bark is crooked, then so is the grain of the heartwood.

Dan had felled a cedar earlier, at a spot just north of Lake Doré, and now we went to collect the wood. He had already halved the felled log and had split one half into quarters. One of these quarters he now split again to form eighths, and he trimmed the bark off with the ax. Then, employing the ax as a cutting edge and wedge, he used an ash maul to drive it into the end in line with the annular rings. Once he had started the split, he twisted

While one son helps split cedar for the gunwales, another wields the ash maul that Dan uses to drive his ax between the annular rings. The cedar quarters can then be pulled apart by hand. (Photo by Denis Alsford, National Museums of Canada.)

the ax by using the haft as a lever until he could grip the separated pieces with his hands to pull them apart manually. As the split progressed, his son Garry stood on the piece to weight it down and add to the leverage. He stood just beyond the extent of the split and gradually moved along the piece until the split was only about 30 cm (1 ft.) from the end. The splitting was done slowly and very carefully to avoid breaking off the wood and to confine the split to the particular annular ring.

Dan split one quarter in this way, inspected the pieces for quality, and trimmed the sides with the ax. One piece had not split too well, and this he halved again lengthwise with a saw. He would use these pieces for ribs and the poorer ones for bows and arrows for the children. The long pieces were 3.6 m (12 ft.) long.

Once sufficient wood had been cut, we carried it to the car, tied it to the sides, and took it back to the workshop. There we stood it on end under a tree, ready for Dan to use.

For the thwarts, Dan usually collected ash immediately prior to their manufacture so that the wood could be used wet, when it was easier to whittle. When making canoes in the

winter, however, he would have to either collect the ash then or use it dry and harder.

We collected ash for the thwarts from beside the road on the reserve. Dan felled a young tree, 12 to 14 cm (5 to 6 in.) in diameter, and Garry and Jeffrey, another son, cut off a 1-m (3-ft.) length with a bucksaw. Dan split this log into two sections, again using the ash maul to drive in the ax. We returned with the wood to the workshop, and Dan started work immediately on the longer center thwarts.

We went out on three occasions to gather spruce roots; twice Dan's sons accompanied us, and on the third trip I acted as his assistant. The only tools Dan brought along were an ax, a jackknife, and a crowbar, which he referred to as a "bent iron."

Dan knew the countryside well and looked for spots where the soil was sandy and only thinly covered with rocks, so that the roots would be close to the surface and easy to get out. Sandy soil also produces better-quality roots that are straighter and of more even thickness. It is also important that the area has not been trampled by cattle, as their feet penetrate the soft soil and can spoil the roots. Dan looked for trees 9 to 12 m (30 to 40 ft.) high, with a clear area around them, so that he could get at the roots easily and to minimize the chances of overlapping by other roots.

Spruce roots are about 10 cm (4 in.) below the surface and tend to radiate out from the tree like spokes of a wheel, but if diverted by a stone or rock they lose their original direction and frequently cross and recross each other. Then extra care needs to be taken in harvesting them, so that a root is not inadvertently broken off.

Dan's method for locating a root was simple. Once a tree was chosen, he dug the crowbar into the soil and dragged through it until it hooked around a root. He pulled upward on the crowbar, exposing the root, and then ripped it out of the soil with his hands. Where it crossed another root, he would examine that root to determine whether it was spruce or some other tree. If it was not spruce, it was cut and left, but if it was spruce and of suitable thickness, then it too was pulled and traced. In this way several roots were exposed at the same time, and it was on occasion like a string puzzle to unravel. Dan worked carefully, not wanting to lose good roots in the process. Occasionally a root would go around or under a large boulder or fallen tree trunk, which we would try to move, and several times by arduous but careful work we were able to obtain roots of 6 m (20 ft.) or more in length.

Sometimes the roots would prove to be too thick or too dry, and we left these. A couple that we gathered subdivided, starting out at about 3 cm (1¼ in.) thick and tapering down to 4.5 mm (³⁄₁₆ in.) thick, all of which was acceptable. The thinner roots would be divided into two pieces for use in sewing splits in the bark skin and sewing the cuts made in the early stages of construction. The thicker roots would be divided into four sections and used for sewing and binding the gunwales and the prows.

We tackled three or four trees, which produced a total of 120 to 150 m (400 to 500 ft.) of binding. The work took about an hour per tree and required considerable strength and energy.

We rolled the bundles and took them back to the house, where Dan put them down in the basement to keep them cool and fresh. To be able to continue work through the winter, a large quantity has to be gathered in the summer, as the winter snows and frozen ground make the task impossible.

To prepare the spruce roots, Dan would bring a bundle from the house to the workshop, untie it, and examine it carefully. Depending on whether the root was to be used for binding the gunwales or sewing up seams, suitable pieces were selected and cut into approximately 1.2-m (4-ft.) lengths. The remainder was then rerolled and returned to the basement.

Dan trimmed off the small side shoots with the jackknife, inserted the blade through the center of the root, and then split it along its length to divide it into two pieces. Once prepared, spruce roots not to be used immediately were kept in the refrigerator. Dan explained that if roots were left in water to keep them supple, they would turn brown, whereas in the refrigerator they remained fresh and white. He stored them wrapped in black polyethylene tied with string. When they were unwrapped, they appeared frosted but thawed quickly and were used immediately. While the spruce roots were being used, Dan kept them in an aluminum pot about half full of water. As he needed a

piece, he would unwind the roots, inspect them for suitability, trim a piece along the width if necessary, and then trim the end of the piece to a point. If the root was thick enough, Dan would divide it again, to create four pieces.

Then, seated, he scraped off the outer bark or skin by placing a pad of cloth over a knee, putting the root inner side down on the pad, and either dragging the root between the knife blade and the pad or scraping it with the knife blade. The inside of the root, which is soft and of no use, he then peeled off, using the point of the blade to separate it from the outer skin. Next, he trimmed the edges to an even width, rolled the piece around three fingers of the left hand into a neat coil, and dropped it into water. Each piece would be made in the same way until Dan felt that he had enough for his immediate needs. He then wrapped the coils and put them into the refrigerator or used them immediately. For the gunwales, he would prepare a large batch, as the roots would be used over a period of several days; much of the rest of the sewing, however, was done immediately after preparing the roots or the next day, so a batch would be prepared as required.

If a root proved to be too dry, Dan would drop it into a bowl of water to soak—cold water if the need was not urgent and could wait until tomorrow, but hot water if the need was immediate. Dan said that hot water would do the work in a few minutes, but cold water could take anywhere from twelve to forty-eight hours. Before Europeans arrived on the scene, Indians would soak the roots in a lake or river or in a birchbark container, or if hot water was necessary, then in a trough made of pine or spruce into which hot stones were dropped.

Once all the materials had been gathered

Dan uses several sizes of awl for canoe building. (Photo by Denis Alsford, National Museums of Canada.)

and prepared, it was time for the preliminary preparations for building the canoe. First Dan tidied and swept the workshop. All the tools were put away into their respective positions, hung on the walls, or laid out on the bench. Miscellaneous materials and waste were either put away or destroyed in the stove. If a completed canoe had not yet been collected by its owner and was still there, then this was put up on the wall on cantilevers to await collection.

For a 3.6-m (12-ft.) canoe, Dan used a bed constructed from planks, already marked out and predrilled to take stakes. This he put up on two sawhorses. Then he laid out on the bench the required stakes, used to support the sides of the canoe in the early stages of manufacture, and checked them for condition. There were fourteen altogether, used in pairs and placed on opposite sides of the canoe at almost regular intervals along its length. These are the outer stakes, of which ten are used in conjunction with inner stakes, which are rectangular in section. The inner stakes are chamfered to a point at one end.

Dan tested the stakes in the holes in the bed to make sure they fit properly, then laid them on the bench in order, ready for use.

The building form, made from plywood, was in two sections. It would be laid on top of the birch bark, and the shape of the canoe would be formed by folding the sides up around it. Dan checked it over to ensure that it was in good condition, as well as the pieces used to hold the two halves in place.

Next, Dan returned to his house to select a piece of birch bark. The rolls of bark had been stored on end on a raised platform to make sure they kept dry. There were six rolls to choose from, and Dan pulled out and measured each one in turn. They were all approximately 1 m (40 in.) wide and, with one exception, long enough for a 3.6-m (12-ft.) canoe, but the thickness varied, as did the markings on the surface that would be the outside of the canoe (the inside of the bark). He took into consideration splits that were visible, marks caused by branches or ax scars, and the general condition of the bark.

After long deliberation, Dan selected a piece, declaring that it would make a fine canoe. This piece was carried to the workshop, where it was untied and laid with the inside of the bark

face down at one end of the bed. A large stone was placed on the bark, and Dan began unrolling it very slowly and carefully, for fear that it might split. When about 1 m (40 in.) had been unrolled, we heard the sound of cracking, so he immediately stopped and got a bucket of hot water. This he poured onto the bark, and then resumed unrolling it.

As he progressed, he weighted down the bark with whatever reasonably heavy object was at hand, a stone or a mallet. Eventually, with a sigh of relief, he unrolled the last of the bark. He wiped off excess water and meticulously picked off loose outer layers from the bark. The cleaning operation took almost three-quarters of an hour.

Then he was ready to center the bark on the bed. He laid the former on top of the bark, surrounding it with odd pieces of timber and weighting it and the bark down with large, heavy rocks. He left it like this for a couple of days.

When work recommenced, Dan removed the lumber and weights surrounding the former, but left the rocks on the former itself. He cut the long sides of the bark at intervals with the jackknife to within a few centimeters

Dan works inside, on a building platform, and pounds the stakes into it. (Photo by Denis Alsford, National Museums of Canada.)

The side panel is selected and fit. (Photo by Denis Alsford, National Museums of Canada.)

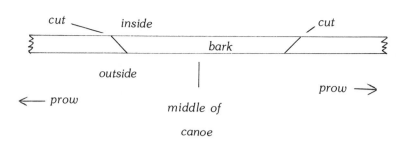

cut ╲   inside   ╲ cut

bark

outside

← prow   prow →

middle of

canoe

The gores in the bark, shown in plan, are cut at angles. (Drawing by Denis Alsford.)

(about 1 in.) of the former in order to make the folding of the sides easier and reduce the chances of cracking or splitting. He determined the number of cuts purely by eye, and on one side made twelve cuts but on the other made ten. In one case, he simply extended an existing split.

From the workshop attic, Dan produced a set of gunwales that he kept for use on the

Then he got some hot water to soften the bark as he bent it.

Starting on side P (see diagram) at the center, he poured hot water onto the bark, bent the side up with his hands, and put the first outer stakes into position, placing a wedge between the stake and the gunwale. He repeated the process on the opposite side, removing the wedge from D just before the side was

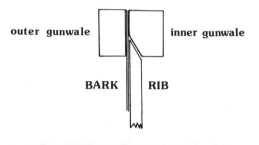

outer gunwale   inner gunwale

BARK   RIB

(Left) The gunwale assembly in cross section: The inner gunwale is cut at an angle to receive the ribs. (Drawing by Denis Alsford.)

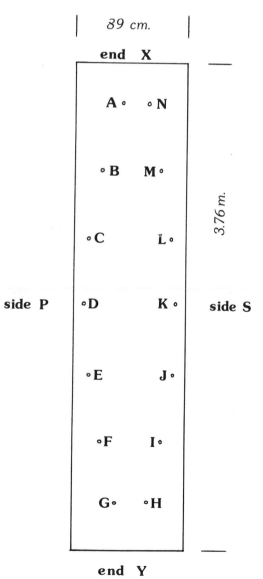

| 89 cm. |

end X

A ∘   ∘ N

∘ B   M ∘

∘ C   L ∘

side P   ∘ D   K ∘   side S

∘ E   J ∘

∘ F   I ∘

G ∘   ∘ H

3.76 m.

end Y

(Left) The side panels are now sewn in place on both sides of the canoe. Dan twists the spruce root as he sews so that the smooth side always faces out. As in all birchbark canoes, the white outer bark of the tree is turned to the inside of the vessel. (Photo by Denis Alsford, National Museums of Canada.)

outside of the canoe to create a sandwich effect, with the bark between the former and gunwales, and the stakes holding it all in place. For now he placed the gunwales on top of the former so that they would be at hand when needed.

Next, he prepared some basswood bark that he took from a tree just outside the workshop, then dropped it into a plastic bowl of water to soak. He placed this bowl on one of the rocks, along with a rib mallet and a claw hammer for driving in the stakes.

He tucked the gunwales under the sides of the canoe, which raised them an inch or so.

The lettered holes of the building platform correspond to the stakes that hold the bark sides upright. (Diagram by Denis Alsford.)

bent up. In this way the bed was held in position so that a complete side could be finished. Returning to the first side (P), Dan poured more water onto the bark and bent the side except for the two end sections at G and A, which he left until side S had been bent up.

Dan then poured a fresh supply of hot water onto end Y, bent the sides up, and inserted two stakes G and H. He followed the same procedure on the opposite end.

He brought in two extra pairs of gunwales to hold up the sides before the inner stakes were positioned and the sides sewn. One pair he put inside the canoe, and the second pair he laid on the bed.

Working from the center on side P, he put the inner stake at D into place, put the gunwales up near the top of the bark, and, after much fiddling, tied the stakes with the basswood binding. Then he placed and tied the inner stake at E, followed by the inner stake at C, then B, then F. He did the same thing on the other side, so that the gunwales were level and locked in place.

In order to raise the prow at this stage, he had to loosen the stake at B and overlap the split between A and B by a few centimeters, with the piece of bark nearest the prow being on the outside. This he repeated on both sides at each end. Then he made a wedge about 7 cm (2³/₄ in.) long and shaped to fit the inside of the lower outer gunwales. These he forced apart, and then inserted the wedges to keep the ends raised.

He now trimmed the ends off roughly to the curve of the prows and placed a large peg low on each prow to hold the bark together.

He pulled old ribs from a pile of miscellaneous pieces of wood and placed these inside and outside the canoe between the stakes to give additional support to the bark above the line of the gunwales at the prows, the stakes at G, H, A, and N tied together with no inner stakes at these points.

Dan continually surveyed his work as he went, looking along the line of the canoe and making minor adjustments until he was completely satisfied. He took no measurements, performing the work entirely by eye. From the time that the bark was uncovered at the edges until this point had taken him three hours of patient work.

The basswood bark was used wet, and as it dried it shrank a little. Once dry, it would retain its shape, so that the inner and outer stakes could be squeezed together with the hand and the binding removed. The necessary work could then be performed and the binding returned to place without the bother of retying it. At this point the canoe was left to dry out while we went to lunch.

After lunch, Dan tidied and swept the workshop in preparation for the next step. He then pulled out a number of what he called "measure sticks." These were in varying lengths and were used to prop up the gunwales while the sides were trimmed and sewn and the gunwales bound.

First, however, Dan prepared some 3-mm (¹/₈-in.) spruce root bindings for sewing the sides, and placed them in a pot of water to keep them supple.

Many of the cuts at the sides overlapped, particularly at the top, and before they could be sewn Dan had to trim them so that they butted up to each other. He inserted the blade of his jackknife at the bottom of the split where there was no overlap, and by working upward he was able to cut both sides of the bark at once and create a perfect joint. He cut the joints at a 45-degree angle to the sides, going against the current at the prow end. He started at one end and gradually worked his way to the other end, removing the stakes as he went. The basswood bindings were still wet, which made it necessary to retie each set. By the following day, however, they had dried out, so that he could just slip the binding off, lay it to one side carefully, and then replace it when he was ready.

When one side had been completed, the other side was done in the same way. Each time he removed a stake, he replaced it very carefully so that the rest of the canoe would not move out of position.

He began sewing the cuts with spruce root at end Y, side S. He sewed the first cut, between stakes H and I, without removing a stake, although he did loosen it briefly in order to remove the rib that was supporting the side at this point. He started at the bottom and worked upward. With an awl, he punched a hole through the bark from the outside, level with the bottom of the split and about 1.25

cm ($\frac{1}{2}$ in.) to one side, and made a second hole on the opposite side of the split and level with the first. Then he selected a piece of spruce root, unrolled it, and trimmed the end to a point. This he pushed through one hole from the inside for about 7 cm ($2\frac{3}{4}$ in.), then back to the inside through the second hole. The holes were always drilled from the outside, and the ends were always on the inside.

A few centimeters above the second hole, he made another hole with the awl. He trimmed the long end, passed it through this hole and over the top of the short end to hold it in place against the side, and pulled the stitching tight. The next hole he made level with the last hole, passed the end through this, and pulled tight. He then punched another pair of holes 2.5 cm (1 in.) above the last and passed the root through as before, so that as the work progressed the sewing appeared as horizontal lines on the outside and diagonal on the inside.

When he reached the top, he passed the end on the inside back and down under the last diagonal and cut it off. The overall effect on the inside was two Xs top and bottom, joined by a series of diagonal lines, while on the outside was a series of neat parallel lines. The inside would later be hidden beneath the lining, but the outside stitching would remain visible in spite of the gumming that would cover it.

A feature of Dan's work was that he always kept in mind the importance of the project's final appearance, but did not allow it to reduce the effectiveness of the operation.

To sew the second seam, the stake at I was removed, and the gunwale was held in place with a temporary spreader bar that was simply an odd piece of wood Dan had trimmed to the required length. This was forced in between the gunwales on either side. The sewing finished directly below the gunwale, which had not been moved from its position. Dan then removed the spreader and I returned the stake to its place. This work continued all the way along one side and back along the other; whenever a stake was in the way, it was removed and the sides wedged as before.

The next step was to adjust the temporary gunwales so that they were approximately level with each other on each side of the canoe and as high as the lowest point of the bark along the side. When they were adjusted to Dan's satisfaction, he made a pencil line along the side the depth of the permanent gunwale above the temporary gunwale and about 60 cm (2 ft.) from each end. This line indicated the point at which the sides of the bark would be trimmed off and the side panels inserted to raise the height of sides.

Dan, again by eye, determined the line that the permanent gunwales would take, and at the appropriate point above the pencil line, he cut the bark with his jackknife down to the level of the temporary gunwales. Starting on side S, end X, he made the first cut then followed suit at end Y and at each end on the other side. Once he had made the initial cuts, he removed the excess bark by running the knife along the bark level with the top of the temporary gunwales, leaving a neat, straight edge. While trimming, he removed any stakes that were in the way one at a time and replaced them as soon as the cutting was completed at that point. Once the cutting had been completed on both sides, he rechecked and readjusted the stakes and temporary gunwales.

In trimming the bark, he had cut through some of the sewing of the splits, but this did not seem to worry him, and he made no attempt to retie the ends. He pointed out that the bark would be sewn along its length, and at those points where the stitching was cut, the ends would be secured by the new sewing.

Dan normally would prefer to cut the extra strips for the sides from one piece, but as he did not have a piece of sufficient length, he used two pieces on each side. Using more than one piece meant that more seams needed to be sewn, but the availability of bark was the governing factor.

Once Dan had found suitable pieces of bark for this purpose, he picked off any odd bits that were loose and used his crooked knife to clean up the outside of the bark. Then he measured the depth he needed and cut it off with the jackknife.

To get the side pieces in place, the stakes had to be removed and the bark forced down between the gunwales. The end that was to butt up to the existing bark was marked, the bark removed and trimmed, replaced, and if it was not a perfect fit, then removed and trimmed again until Dan was perfectly satisfied. The next strip was then cut and fitted in much the same way, until the gap was filled and all the pieces fit snugly. Once a piece was in position to his satisfaction, he returned the stakes to their places.

After the side pieces were in position, they were sewn to the main piece of bark. The stakes were loosened and the temporary gunwales raised to a position approximately 2.5 cm (1 in.) above the line of the edge of the main bark skin. To keep the additional pieces from curling up on the inside, some old ribs were put in between the inner stakes and the bark.

Using the point of the square awl and a piece of wood as a straightedge, Dan scribed a line along the outside as a guide for sewing, 1.25 cm ($\frac{1}{2}$ in.) below the level of the main bark where the inserts were placed.

Dan prepared spruce roots 3 mm ($\frac{1}{8}$ in.) wide. Then, using the triangular awl, he punched the first hole through from the outside, starting at one end and 18.75 mm ($\frac{3}{4}$ in.) before the joint started. He pushed the root through until there was an equal length on each side, and then made the next hole a few centimeters farther along. The outside length of the root was passed through this hole first, and the inside length was twisted 180 degrees before being passed out through the same hole, but slightly above the outside length of root, the hole being enlarged if necessary to accommodate it. The twisting was necessary so that the rougher side of the spruce root would not show on the outside of the canoe. The rough side of the root would be showing on the inside, but this would be completely hidden later by the lining. Only one twist was needed, for the root would continue to face the same way in the succeeding holes.

When Dan got to the end of the first length of root, he tied it on the inside with an over-and-under tie and trimmed the ends. He put the next piece of root through the last hole used to maintain continuity, and sewed it in the same manner as the first piece. As Dan reached a stake, he would remove it, returning it to its place when he was well past. This process continued until the side was completed.

For this canoe, Dan would make 3.75-m-long (12$\frac{1}{2}$-ft.-long) gunwales for the inside and outside. The inner gunwale would be 16 mm ($\frac{5}{8}$ in.) wide by 22 mm ($\frac{7}{8}$ in.) deep, and the outer gunwale 10 mm ($\frac{3}{8}$ in.) wide by 22 mm ($\frac{7}{8}$ in.) deep.

He had several pieces of cedar available for the gunwales, leaning up against a tree in the shade. He took some time in selecting a piece, examining the wood carefully to see that the grain was straight and even and that there were no knots or blemishes. He brought the chosen piece into the workshop, laid the edge of his jackknife blade along the line where he wanted to split it, and tapped the blade with the rib mallet. He then withdrew the blade and inserted the ax in the impression left, tapped the ax with the maul, and twisted the ax blade just a little to open up a split for about 30 cm (1 ft.). He then split the rest with his hands.

He did the splitting very carefully. Using his knee to push against the side of the strip just beyond the extent of the split, he would continue to pull the two pieces apart to just beyond his knee, then move the whole thing along and repeat the process until he had the two pieces separated.

Then he sat on a stool and, using the crooked knife, began to whittle a piece down to its required size, 3.8 to 4.5 cm. (1$\frac{1}{2}$ to 1$\frac{3}{4}$ in.) deep by 19 mm ($\frac{3}{4}$ in.) thick. Both pairs were sawn off to the right length, and then the ends were tapered, the outer pair only a little on the depth and not on the thickness, but the inner pair on both depth and thickness. Dan notched the ends so that the gunwales could be tied around the end piece once all were in place and before the last sewing at the ends of the gunwales were done.

When completed, the inner pair was tied together with basswood around the notched ends, and Dan marked a line with a pencil at the center point. On either side of this line, he drew another line 2.54 cm (1 in.) away and marked a green cross in each resulting triangle to indicate where the thwarts were to go. Then, working toward one end, he drew additional lines across the two gunwales, leaving a 3.8-cm (1$\frac{1}{2}$-in.) gap next, followed by a 5.08-cm (2-in.) gap, then a 3.8-cm (1$\frac{1}{2}$-in.) gap, then a 5.08-cm (2-in.) gap, and so on until the tip was reached. The 5.08-cm (2-in.) gaps indicated the areas to be bound, except for two more 5.08-cm (2-in.) gaps that were marked off in green pencil to indicate the positions of the center and end thwarts.

He then removed the inner stakes on one side, took out the temporary gunwales and replaced them with the permanent gunwales, then replaced the stakes. He adjusted the gunwales by loosening the stakes in turn and by using measuring sticks raised to their proper heights. He used 22.86-cm (9-in.) measuring sticks at the center and longer ones up to 26 cm (10¹/₄ in.) long toward the ends. The other side was done in the same way.

At this point, the bark along the sides extended beyond the tops of the gunwales. Using the jackknife, Dan trimmed this level with the top of the gunwales between the stakes, but left the excess bark where the stakes were for fear that the gunwales would move again.

The gunwales were now lashed into place with spruce root bindings. Dan started next to the center stakes to get the gunwales fixed, binding the sections on either side of the stakes and on both sides of the canoe first.

He began by selecting, inspecting, and trimming a piece of spruce root, cutting the ends to a point. Then he forced the inner gunwale and the bark with the jackknife blade, and inserted the end of the root in the gap next to the left-hand line and between the other line 5.08 cm (2 in.) away, which was the direction that the binding would take. The root was then wrapped around the outer gunwale.

He pushed a hole through the bark directly underneath the gunwale, passed the root through this hole to the inside, and drew it tight, so that the outside root was vertical. Then he passed the root around both gunwales working toward the right, pushed another hole through the bark with the awl, passed the root through, and drew it tight again. The outside roots were kept vertical, while on the inside they slanted. This kept the outside looking neater.

This method of binding was continued until the space between the two drawn lines 5.08 cm (2 in.) apart was filled. Dan next did those on either side of the intermediate thwart positions, followed by the ones on either side of the end thwart positions. Then he did every other one in the gaps between the thwarts, leaving the remainder, except for the thwart bindings and those at the prows, for his wife to do.

Once the wrapping had been completed, Dan pushed the root through in and out under the gunwale, back along the length of the wrapping. The last time he passed it through to the inside, it was trimmed off. He passed it back this way through every other hole made for the wrapping, extending the holes to allow this.

After Dan removed the stakes to allow the binding to continue, he put measuring sticks under the gunwales to keep them in place, and also used a store-bought steel clamp to hold them. The clamps were used particularly at the prow ends, where the gunwales were being forced up in line with the slope of the prow.

At this point Dan decided to make the end piece and fit it. Dan preferred to use what he called natural crook cedar for the stem-piece. This was a piece of cedar that in its natural shape suited the prow end of the canoe, and all it required from Dan was some whittling. If he could not find a suitable piece, he made the stem-piece from straight-grained cedar, bending it to the required shape.

To make a piece from straight cedar, the method was as follows: Dan would select a piece, paying particular attention to the straightness of the grain. He would cut it to the required length, about 60 cm (2 ft.) long, then use the crooked knife to trim it. For most of its length it was made roughly diamond shaped, but the last 7.6 cm (3 in.) were left rectangular. The rectangular end was the top at the point where the stem-piece would be lashed to the gunwales. From the opposite end, he split the piece with the jackknife. The first cut was started in the center of the end and went down into the thick section about 15 cm (6 in.). Next, he split the piece again midway between the first split and the edge on the

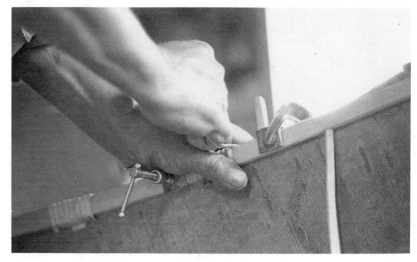

Clamps hold the inwale and outwale tight while the lashing proceeds. (Photo by Denis Alsford, National Museums of Canada.)

opposite half. Then each section was halved again and again, until the stem-piece had been split fifteen times. Each section at this point was about 3 mm (1/8 in.) thick.

Dan then steamed and bent the stem-piece around his knee as he had with the ribs, and lashed it round and round with basswood. He tied the ends to one another to prevent the piece from straightening, and then left it to dry in the sun for a day or so. The basswood binding served two purposes: to act as a clamp on the split sections and stop them from straightening out, and to keep the end piece from splitting when holes were made for the lashings that would hold it in place at the prow.

With natural crook cedar, the need to steam and bend—the most tricky part of the operation—is eliminated, which also saves a couple of days of drying time plus time spent on manufacture.

With a natural crook end, once Dan had whittled the piece to the desired shape and bound it with basswood, he tried it in place, and then marked with a pencil the line that the top of the inner gunwale took across it. Then he removed it and waisted the top end to take the gunwales. With a saw or a knife, he made a cut that went down to the depth of the flat section at the front and back of the piece. He turned it over and did the same thing on the other side, and then repeated the process 5 cm (2 in.) below each cut and parallel to them. These cuts were at a slight angle to the horizontal to allow for the slope of the prow at that point. With a chisel, he gouged out the wood between the cuts, and the end piece was then ready to be fitted into place.

He put the stem-piece into position, trimming the inner gunwales slightly to make a good fit. Next, he made a tapered peg from a piece of cedar 10 cm (4 in.) long. He punched a hole with the awl directly beneath the gunwale at a point three-quarters of the way back from the leading edge of the piece, and inserted the peg, which served to hold the stem-piece in place and support the gunwales at the desired height.

The next step was to sew the stem-piece into place temporarily with basswood, starting at the bottom and working toward the top. The first three holes were drilled at 19-mm (3/4-in.) intervals, and the remainder at 3.8- to 5-cm (1 1/2- to 2-in.) intervals until the top was reached. The temporary basswood binding was stitched in a similar way to the sewing used on the extra pieces of bark added to the sides—it was passed through the first hole until the same amount was on each side, then passed through the next hole up on one side, then the other side, then up to the next hole, and so on to the top, where it was tied.

Once the end piece was thus sewn in, Dan very carefully trimmed off the bark to match the line of the end piece, taking great care to avoid cutting the basswood binding around the stem-piece.

According to Dan, the manboard was the old way of fitting a stem-piece. A manboard serves to ensure that the stem-piece is in correctly and square on to the line of the canoe. The manboard has to fit the sides of the canoe snugly to allow for the lining. The shoulders also serve to support the gunwales in the right position. When he used a manboard, he would try the stem-piece and manboard fitted together in place, and mark the point where the inner gunwales would go. Then he would carve out this section, forming the shoulders for the head, which was carved next. When this was all done, either the whole thing was sewn into place as described before, or the manboard was split out bit by bit (it cannot come out in one piece because of the way it fits around the gunwales and the stem-piece at the bottom). It is left in or taken our depending on the style of the canoe.

Now the remaining binding of the gunwales, except for the thwart section, was done by Dan's wife, Bernadette, while he prepared some ribs. In this case, she would be binding the prow ends, and both sets of gunwales would be bound at the same time.

Bernadette started the binding by tucking the end of the root in between the bark and the inner gunwale so that the root started level with the back of the stem-piece. With the awl, she then punched a hole just behind the end piece and out through the other side of the canoe in the other piece of bark. The root was passed through and up and over the other side, and back across the top of both sets of gunwales down the side. She punched the next set of holes and repeated the process. She continued in this manner until the root wrapped both sets of gunwales three times at one end and twice at the other. The next wrap around went over only the first set of gunwales, then passed down below the opposite side and came out beneath them, passing back over the top and down inside to the other side again, continuing until ten or eleven wraps had been done.

Then she tucked the end of the root under the top of the last binding and cut off the excess. This would eventually be hidden by the upper gunwale when it was fitted at a later stage. This binding would serve not only to hold the gunwales in place, but also to hold the two sides together at the prows.

While she had been working on the ends, she had removed the prow stakes and then replaced them when an end was completed. Now, their job finished, all the inner stakes were removed and put to one side.

The next stage was the manufacture and fitting of the thwarts. The thwarts were made from ash that was used green, in fact as soon as possible after cutting, when it was easier to whittle. We collected the ash in the early afternoon, and as soon as we returned to the workshop, Dan took one of the half sections and split it into two to make quarters. All the pieces of ash he kept in the workshop out of the sun.

He peeled the bark off one quarter and split out the heartwood with the ax. He then sawed the piece to a length of 81.28 cm (32 in.), which was the distance that one bark side would be from the other at the center of the canoe. The ash was first whittled down to the right width and thickness, and the sides rounded off. Then Dan marked off the ends at the sides, made a saw cut approximately 13 mm ($\frac{1}{2}$ in.) deep on each side, and whittled the ends with the crooked knife to produce a waist. Both ends had previously been tapered, so that the piece appeared to be rectangular from above but tapered from the side.

When the ends had been waisted, Dan eyed the piece and whittled off small bits until he was satisfied that it was smooth and regular.

The end thwarts were also carved from ash but were much shorter, had a distinct curve, and were of an even width.

Once made, the thwarts were immediately fitted. First, Dan cut slots or mortises out of the inner gunwales at a spot he had marked with a pencil. Green crosses on the top of the gunwales indicated the place, and he dropped a vertical line to just below the half of the depth

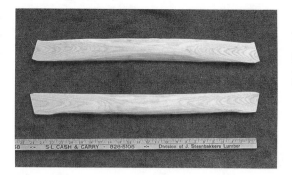

The thwarts are whittled from green ash. Note that the intermediate thwarts taper in thickness only. (Photo by Denis Alsford, National Museums of Canada.)

of the gunwale at each end of the marked line across the gunwale. Then he marked two dots on these lines to indicate the thickness of the thwart and drew lines across to join them up. With a gouge, he cut out the resulting triangle, starting at each end and working in toward the middle and to the depth of the bark. He cleaned out the slot with the jackknife and tried the thwart for fit. Then he did the same on the other side. When both sides fit perfectly, he took out the two end pairs of stakes and pressed the thwart home into position. This was managed with a struggle, as the prow was sewn together and there was not a great deal of play to allow the thwart to get in. Once this was accomplished, they were bound into place with spruce roots.

First, four pencil marks were made flush to the side of the inner gunwale along the thwart,

The center thwart is installed before the intermediate thwarts because it spreads the the gunwales slightly, reducing the depth of the canoe. (Photo by Denis Alsford, National Museums of Canada.)

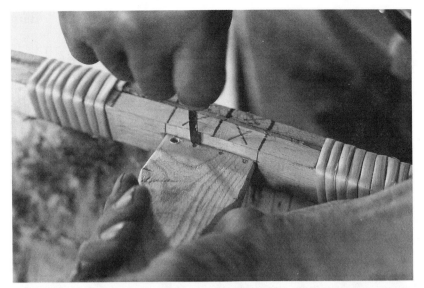

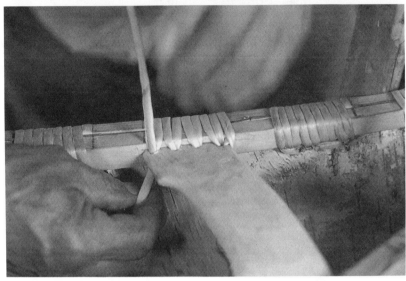

(Top) *Holes are drilled in the center thwart to receive the lashing. (Photo by Denis Alsford, National Museums of Canada.)*

(Bottom) *The end thwarts, cut in a slight curve, are laced in place. (Photo by Denis Alsford, National Museums of Canada.)*

the next hole through the bark, and passed the root through and up through the second hole in the thwart. On this hole and the next hole, he passed the root through twice; on the last hole he passed it through a third time, then passed it back underneath the thwart and pushed it out through the bark. Then he pushed it in and out alternate holes in the bark, finally cutting it off on the inside, in much the same way as the gunwales had been finished off. He followed the same procedure for the other side of the thwart. When completed, Dan tested it by trying to pull the sides apart with his hands. Then he put in the thwart at the other prow end in the same way.

Once he had finished, he removed the stones holding the canoe down and, with a claw hammer, drew out the nails holding the two halves of the former together. He lifted the former clear of the bottom of the canoe to make sure it was free, then dropped it back in place and replaced the central stone.

Now the end stakes (outer) were replaced and the center stakes removed to fit the center thwart. Dan cut the mortises in the inner gunwales as before, bound them, and put in the thwarts. Before binding, however, he measured to determine the length that the other pair of thwarts, which were to go midway between the center and the other thwarts, would need to be.

When the center thwart was in place, it was obvious that both prows had risen by 5 cm (2 in.). Dan pointed out that if he had left the former as it was while sewing the thwart in place, he would have had great difficulty in getting the former out later, and the heavy stones at the ends would have made it difficult for the prows to rise.

Dan then started on the last pair of thwarts. He used the remaining half of the ash piece, splitting this in half again with the ax and maul. He sawed it off to the required length of 66.35 cm (26½ in.), trimmed the bark off with the ax, and split off the heartwood. He then split off another piece 19 mm (¾ in.) thick tapering to 2.54 cm (1 in.) thick, and he trimmed this with the ax to roughly the desired measurements, carefully tapering the ends. Then he finished it with the crooked knife, treating the width, thickness, and edges, and checked the work by eye.

Before he fitted the thwart, he found an odd scrap of cedar under his bench, which he

two of them near the leading and trailing edge, and the other two at equal distances apart in between. Using the gouge, Dan then cut these out to make holes for the binding.

He passed the end of the root through the first hole in the thwart from the underside, exposing about an inch. This end was held against the side of the inner gunwale, and the long part of the root was brought up from underneath and over the top of the gunwales, trapping the short end of the root as it went against the side of the inner gunwale. Then Dan punched a hole through the bark with an awl from the outside and in line with the edge of the thwart. He pushed the root through and pulled it tight, passed it up through the first hole in the thwart again, and wrapped it around the gunwales. He punched another hole through the bark with the awl, pushed the root through this, and drew it tight again. He then pushed it up through the first hole yet again, passed it around the gunwales, punched sawed off to a length of 63 cm (25 in.). This he used as a spreader by wedging it from side to side between the gunwales, 10 cm (4 in.) in front of the position that the thwart was to take. He laid the freshly carved thwart across the canoe in the position it was to take but on top of the gunwales, and using a piece of wood as a straightedge, he penciled a line that took the same line as the inside of the bark. He did so on both sides and trimmed the thwart with the saw to the line so that it was exactly right. Further trimming of the thwart was then carried out with the crooked knife; in particular, the sides were trimmed to waist them near the ends on one side.

Throughout the afternoon, Bernadette carried on with binding the gunwale sections that Dan had left untouched.

The following morning, the two intermediate thwarts were placed in position. Dan circled the canoe looking along its length, checking that the canoe was taking its proper shape and that it was symmetrical. Then we talked while the roots that Dan had brought out from the refrigerator thawed. Once the roots were ready, the binding was done as before.

Dan then took out the large stone from the center of the former, and removed the former, which had to be lifted at the center and then slid out toward one end. Then he removed all the remaining stakes and the canoe was free.

Dan now cleaned up the inside of the bark, picking off most of the silver bark to expose the salmon pink of the bark beneath. He swept the inside of the canoe clean, then turned the canoe upside down and closely inspected it.

Four stakes were driven into the bed in

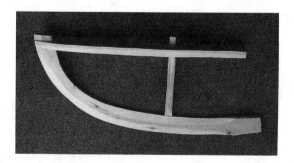

holes already prepared for them, 8.75 cm (3½ in.) from the side of the bed and 1.11 m (3 ft. 8 in.) from the ends. A nail was driven into each stake 35.56 cm (14 in.) above the bed, and when driven into the bed the stakes were in line with the intermediate thwarts. The nail

was on the outside of the stake, and a basswood binding was placed around the intermediate thwarts on the underside, then passed around the stake and over the top of the nail, so that the canoe was lifted 3.8 cm (1½ in.) clear of the bed. This would allow room for the bottom of the canoe to round out when the ribs were put in and driven home.

The thirty-eight ribs necessary for this canoe were made at odd moments when Dan could not proceed on the current work on the canoe. Dan would split the ribs with an ax and maul from cedar stock that he had stored outside in the shade of trees or in the workshop. The sections ranged from 17.78 by 17.78 cm (7 by 7 in.) to 10.16 by 5.08 cm (4 by 2 in.), into pieces 8.6 cm (3⅜ in.) wide by 13 to 19 mm (½ to ¾ in.) thick.

For the ribs, a length of white cedar is cut in a particular sequence: perpendicular to the bark in halves, quarters, and eighths, then a fourth cut parallel to the bark. The resulting piece is further cut into more riblike proportions. (Photo by Denis Alsford, National Museums of Canada.)

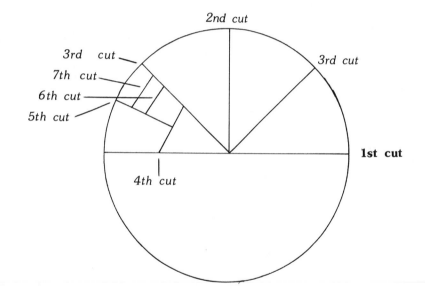

After splitting twenty to thirty pieces, he took up his crooked knife, put a blanket on top of a cedar log, sat down, and began to whittle. He tapered the ends at the edges about 38 cm (15 in.) from the end, reducing the width to about 2.54 cm (1 in.). He then trimmed the thickness to 13 mm (½ in.). From that stage on, he just kept whittling off a bit here and a bit there, frequently holding the rib up to look along its length until he was satisfied with it. He then braced it against his knee to see if it would bend evenly, and if not happy he would trim a little more off until he was perfectly satisfied. He finished by rounding off the edges, then began on the next piece.

He stored the finished ribs under the bench until needed. When he was ready to use the

Dan fits the stem-piece to the manboard with a support strut. (Photo by Denis Alsford, National Museums of Canada.)

Dan carves the cedar battens with his crooked knife. (Photo by Denis Alsford, National Museums of Canada.)

To mark where the ribs should be bent, Dan measures with his fingers: four fingers from the inwale at the center, three at the intermediate thwarts, two at the ends. (Photo by Denis Alsford, National Museums of Canada.)

them out in order. He collected odd pieces of plywood and thin strips of wood from various corners of the workshop, and placed these in the bottom of the canoe. These were to be used as temporary lining while the ribs were being bent and were drying out in the canoe.

Dan wedged sticks under the gunwales and down to the floor of the canoe to hold the strips in position and to help push the bottom down or out. Then the canoe was lifted off the sawhorses and put down onto the floor, and Dan replaced the ribs in pairs as before. He then used a piece of charcoal to mark the ribs at the point where they were to be bent.

ribs, he pulled them out and laid them in pairs across the canoe, the long ones near the center and the shorter ones toward the end.

Dan said that the correct procedure in building a canoe was to make all the ribs and gunwales first, but he had never done it that way. Perhaps, he mused, because he was too impatient and wanted to get the bark laid out and in position.

It seemed to me that there was no real reason to taper the ribs at each end, so I asked Dan why he bothered with this additional work. He replied that it cut down on the weight of the canoe at the sides, whereas at the bottom the canoe needed more strength.

He now took the ribs off the canoe and laid

The building frame has been removed, and Dan can remove excess bark. (Photo by Denis Alsford, National Museums of Canada.)

The bending was started in the morning, first thing, and Dan hoped to have them all bent by midday, but was prepared for difficulties, particularly on the end ribs, which had a single very sharp bend.

He now lighted the stove and brought out an old gas tank from a Model-T Ford. This he filled about one-third with water and put on the stove. Once the water began to boil, steam issued from a hole at one end of the tank. He put the central pairs of ribs into the hole so that they were above the water in the steam, and blocked the open part of the hole with a rag.

The ribs remained in the steam for three or four minutes. Dan then took out a pair and bent it by putting the spot marked with charcoal against his knee and pulling the ends toward him. Then he looped a piece of stout string around the middle and drew it tight. This served to hold the bend in place, and he returned the rib pair to the tank, with the other end inside this time.

The second pair was taken out, treated in the same manner, and returned to the tank. About a minute later, Dan again took the first pair from the tank and bent the other end around his knee. Then he slipped the string loose and moved it up to the tip. Holding the ends of the ribs, Dan put them into place in the canoe and removed the string altogether. Those ribs were then left to set, as he removed the third pair from the top of the canoe and put them into the tank. For the rest of the ribs, he followed the same procedure as with the first pair, gradually working toward the prows of the canoe.

After he had put the second pair into the canoe, he nailed a rough crossbar to the gunwale across the canoe between the center thwart and the intermediate thwart on each end in order to prevent the ribs from bowing the sides and gunwales as they tried to straighten while drying.

The workshop became extremely hot and Dan was very anxious in case a rib cracked as he bent it. From time to time he would inspect those ribs that were already placed and pushed them down into the canoe as they attempted to rise out like a cork from a bottle.

As the pairs were bent and placed, the distance between the bends grew smaller and the space for inserting them was also more confined, and the bending became far more critical. When only one pair remained to be placed at each end, Dan nailed another rough crossbar across between the intermediate and end thwarts.

Once the last pairs at each end were bent, they were placed in a different manner. Dan held them at the top with one hand and passed them through under the end thwart from the center and up above the line of the gunwales, pushing the bottoms of the ribs into place with his hand. He also bent and placed the last single prow rib. He broke three ribs during this whole process and immediately made new ribs to replace them.

When all the ribs were in place, he carefully took out the top rib of each pair, turned it around, and put it into its proper place in the gap next to the one it had originally been in. Toward the prows he had to drive the ribs home with the rib mallet. When they were all in place, he wedged them using odd pieces of wood and an extra pair of shorter gunwales. These were held in place with lengths of wood that Dan cut to length as he went, to act as wedges across the width of the canoe. The canoe was left until the next day to allow the ribs to dry.

The following morning, the ribs were sawed off level with the gunwales. Starting at one end, Dan cut off the first rib with a saw held so that the handle was above the level of the gunwales and the tip of the blade, on the inside of the canoe, was below the level of the gunwales. He took care to avoid cutting the bindings on the gunwales.

Two pairs of ribs are ready at the center thwart. (Photo by Denis Alsford, National Museums of Canada.)

The rib ends are tied to retain the bend. (Photo by Denis Alsford, National Museums of Canada.)

Occasionally a rib would be straightened. Dan completed both sides in this manner.

The next step was to prepare the lining. The lining material was taken from the cedar directly beneath the bark. Dan cut this material into 11-cm-wide (4^1/$_3$-in.-wide) strips.

On the floor beside the canoe was a trough made by cutting a cylindrical water tank in half. This was three-quarters filled with water, and the strips that Dan had cut were placed in the trough and weighted down with a large stone.

While these were soaking, Dan started on the first piece of lining. This piece needed to be thicker at the front and stronger than the other pieces, as it would be placed at the part of the canoe that was most vulnerable when in use.

Dan did most of the shaping with the crooked knife, but he did a lot of work on the underside with a plane. The top side was hollowed out and the underside was trimmed so that the edges were quite sharp. The front end underneath was left thicker and fell away from the tip at quite an angle.

At this time, the wedges and temporary gunwales on the inside of the canoe were removed to free the ribs. Dan numbered all the ribs, then, starting at the center, he removed them as well as the temporary lining.

The sheathing pieces are laid in an overlapping pattern, like roofing shingles. (Photo by Denis Alsford, National Museums of Canada.)

Now Dan trimmed the rib ends in preparation for their final fitting, tapering the sides at the ends and then beveling the tips to a sharp point. The points would be pushed up under the inner gunwale, which had been beveled to take the ribs before it was fitted.

He now removed the slings from the stakes and the stakes themselves, and placed a blanket underneath each end of the canoe to act as a cushion. Then shorter stakes were put into the bed at the end holes to prevent the canoe from moving.

Upon close inspection of the bark skin, Dan discovered a very bad split, about 15 cm (6 in.) long, which would first have to be sewn. He removed the stakes, inverted the canoe, and stitched the split.

Dan next applied duct tape to some smaller splits, places that he thought showed signs of weakness, and the split that had been sewn. In the old days, Dan said, this patching would have been done with deerskin stuck on with spruce gum. The tape used for patching would not show once the canoe was finished.

The first piece of lining material that Dan had prepared was now inserted into the canoe. Its tip went under the bottom and trailing edge of the end piece, and Dan put a wedge from the end thwart down to the lining so that it

would not move about. Then the corresponding piece at the other end was put in.

Dan removed the stones from the trough so that the lining pieces floated free, and as he required a piece he just took it off the top of the pile. He took the first piece out of the trough and proceeded to taper one end at one side, round the other end, and thin the edge to a point. The tapered end he also pointed in the same way. The tapering was done so that the piece would fit snugly along the side of the end piece, and Dan tried it in position several times before he was satisfied that it would fit properly. When it was ready, he placed it in position and cut and tucked a thin strip of the lining material into the canoe as a rib to temporarily hold the lining pieces in place until the ribs proper were ready to go in.

Dan positioned the second piece of lining at the "corner" of the bottom of the canoe, randomly up the side. The next two lining pieces to be made and added were placed above this second piece to form the sides, and they were cut to fit alongside the end piece and

rounded at the opposite end. The bottom edge of each overlapped the top edge of the piece below.

The other side of the canoe was then done in the same way, before the gaps at the bottom were filled. When doing the filling, Dan took care to overlap the pieces in the same pattern as the other pieces. The ends at the center of the canoe were not level, but this was not important. The top piece of lining did not fit tightly under the gunwale; a gap of 1.9 cm (^{3}/$_4$ in.) was left.

Before all the filling had been completed, after the three pieces on the bottom were in, the lining completely covered the floor and sides for approximately 30 cm (1 ft.), and at this point Dan removed the wedge holding the first lining piece and put in the first three ribs. The second one split as it went in, but Dan left it. He then drove the ribs home with a blue oak rib mallet and a driver that he had fashioned from cedar. The rib driver had to made of the same material as the ribs in order not to mark them. At this time the ribs were not vertical, and Dan would drive them home to the upright position over a period to allow the bark time to stretch and prevent its splitting.

When the gaps had been completely filled, the remaining ribs were put in, so that twelve ribs now were in place. Dan had some difficulty getting some of the ribs under the gunwales on both sides at the same time. When this happened, he would cut an odd piece of wood to length and wedge it across the tops of the rib to force them out; then he would drive them home.

The work was tricky and at times exasperating. On one occasion the lining slipped out of position, and Dan had to remove a couple of ribs to get the lining back into place before carrying on.

Once he had finished, he swept the inside of the canoe, and then turned the canoe around end for end. Then it was turned upside down and inspected. The end where the ribs had been fitted was now rounding out, and the difference between the two ends was very obvious. Dan was satisfied with his progress, so the canoe was righted again.

He then followed the same procedure on the other end, the two ends taking up the major part of a day's work. Before leaving the canoe overnight, Dan put down a piece of unprepared lining in the center of the canoe bottom and put in a wedge under the center gunwale to help press the bottom down and out overnight. He also tied the remaining ribs across the ends to keep them from straightening out.

The following morning, he cut and placed the lining in the middle section of the canoe. Dan worked on the center piece first and progressed along alternate sides, gradually working up the sides to just below the gunwales again. Along the edges, the overlapping was as before, with the lower edge of one piece overlapping the upper edge of the piece below. But the ends overlapped the corresponding piece at each end of the canoe, but were in turn overlapped by the pieces on either side of it.

The temporary ribs of cedar were used to keep the lining in place and were removed when the proper ribs were put in. Dan now put in the remaining ribs except for two, which were left for later. It was not possible to get these two ribs in at this stage because of the angle that the other ribs took, and Dan would have to wait to install them until the rest had been driven home and upright.

In driving home the larger ribs at the center, Dan would tap them first in the center at the bottom, then at the sides, in this way easing them home along their length and evenly distributing the strain put on them. He closely inspected the sides of the canoe at frequent intervals to make sure no splits were developing. He now had to use a short and a long driver, as he had to work around the thwarts; at the prow ends, the long one was particularly useful.

When all the ribs had been driven home as far as possible at this time, Dan once again turned the canoe upside down, inspected it, thumped it with his fist, and declared it satisfactory. The last two ribs he tied across the ends and hung up for later fitting.

Now it was time to start fitting the gunwale caps. Dan made these at the same time as the inner and outer gunwales, tied them together with basswood binding, and placed them in the lake under a piece of flat iron. When he removed them from the water, they were a light brown, but when untied, the sides that had been together were still white. He had not narrowed the ends at all, but he had hollowed the underside of each gunwale, so that when they were put in position along the tops of the other gunwales, the new ones would not only

The gunwale cap is nailed and pegged. (Photo by Denis Alsford, National Museums of Canada.)

cover them but would also better fit the slight curve created by the bindings.

Iron nails 5 cm (2 in.) long were used to secure the gunwale caps in position. Starting at the center of the canoe, Dan drove one nail into each gap between the bindings at an angle with the gunwale, going in on one side above the inner gunwale and out toward the outer gunwale in the direction of the inner gunwale. He left all the nails projecting by about 6 mm, so that they could easily be withdrawn later when it was time to put in the permanent nails.

He positioned a finger-tightened C-clamp just ahead of the nailing immediately being done, to hold the gunwale cap in place as he worked. When he reached the point where the intermediate thwart was positioned, Dan worked back along toward the other end of the canoe. As work progressed, it became more and more difficult to hold the gunwale in place, and he had to use the clamp with cloth guards over the faces to avoid marking the gunwale.

When Dan reached the sixth rib, he trimmed the gunwale with the jackknife to fit around the end piece, and then tapered it to take the other gunwale when that was placed in position. This free end he hooked over the end piece. He then proceeded to do the opposite end in the same way. When this end was completed, it too was hooked over the end

piece, and Dan then followed the same procedure with the gunwale on the opposite side. He was very worried that these might split.

Once he had finished the trimming for the stem-piece, he sawed all the gunwales off to a uniform length and trimmed the gunwale caps to fit properly with one another and around the stem-piece. Then these were nailed in position.

The ends had been very difficult, for the bend of the prows both upward and inward had put great stress on the gunwales. I helped Dan at this time, although normally he would have managed on his own with the use of C-clamps. He preferred not to use these, however, for fear of marking the gunwales.

Dan next used the rib mallet and drivers to drive the ribs that were already in place home further. He started at the prows and worked toward the center, moving each one 13 to 19 mm ($^1/_2$ to $^3/_4$ in.).

One of the two remaining ribs was now taken down from where it had been hanging on a nail on the wall, the string holding it in shape untied, and the rib put into place and tapped in. This left only one rib to go in, but this would have to wait until all the other ribs were upright, because there was not sufficient room in the bottom of the canoe to get it in at this time.

Inspection of the underside of the canoe showed that the joints along the sides were tending to pull apart as they tightened. This did not worry Dan, however, and he did not see any real danger of the canoe splitting asunder. At the seam where the extra bark had been added to the sides of the canoe, the bark had pulled away from its original place by 3 mm.

Dan now took a piece of cedar that was leaning against the side of the workshop and split off a piece with his jackknife so that it was 1.9 cm ($^3/_4$ in.) by 2.54 cm (1 in.) in cross section, then sawed this into 10-cm (4-in.) lengths. He split one of these pieces in half lengthwise, and from one of these halves he made a nail that tapered to a point at one end and remained roughly square at the other. He then polished and slightly compressed the nail by scraping it with the blade of the knife held at right angles to the nail. He proceeded to make eighty such nails.

When they were all ready, he started to put them in, beginning at the center of the canoe. He would first withdraw an iron nail with a

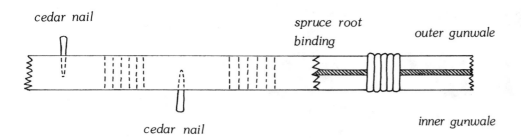

cedar nail

spruce root binding

outer gunwale

cedar nail

inner gunwale

In plan: the gunwale cap covers the inwale and outwale with its filling of bark. (Diagram by Denis Alsford.)

claw hammer and use the square awl to enlarge the hole. Next, he would drive a wooden nail in with the rib mallet, so that it projected out through the lower gunwales by about 13 mm (¹/₂ in.). Then he cut off the head and the exposed point flush with the jackknife.

During this process, as well as during the manufacture of the nails, Dan took a couple of breaks to drive the ribs home further, each time moving them approximately 6 mm (¹/₄ in.). Dan pointed out that the ribs could not be hurried; the bark needed time to stretch each time the ribs were moved.

By the time the nailing process was completed, the ribs were almost upright. The remaining rib was now taken down from where it was hanging on the wall and untied. Dan had great difficulty getting this rib into position in the canoe. He tried it first from the side of the canoe that the rib belonged on, then from the other side, passing it under the center thwart. He put a wedge across the canoe from side to side to force it open a bit, and finally he thought he would be able to make it. He eventually managed to get it within 2.54 cm (1 in.) of its proper position, using the short driver to help.

The canoe was then turned upside down, and Dan tapped the bark skin so that the bits and pieces of debris fell out. He lifted the canoe at one end and put a sawhorse under it, then swept the bed clean.

With the canoe still upside down, Dan trimmed the bark at the bottom to produce a stepped effect that would allow a piece of spruce root to be inserted into the first hole. He carefully selected a piece of spruce root for its straightness and width; this root had to be the same width as the two bark sides and the leading edge of the end piece. He trimmed the end of the root to a pointed wedge and inserted it in the gap just cut. Then he wrapped the root around the front of the canoe and cut it off, leaving enough to tuck up under and

between the inner gunwales. Dan said that this spruce root frontal piece was called a bunting iron on modern canoes.

At the bow the bark is trimmed and made ready for finishing. (Photo by Denis Alsford, National Museums of Canada.)

Stem batten covers the stem-piece. (Photo by Denis Alsford, National Museums of Canada.)

The inboard view of the bow and stem-piece shows the neat lacing of the spruce root. (Photo by Denis Alsford, National Museums of Canada.)

The basswood binding that was around the front was then cut near the top. Dan selected a piece of spruce root binding a few centimeters wide and made a hole with the awl 2.54 cm (1 in.) in from the edge and 13 mm. (¹/₂ in.) from toward the prow from where the bark had just been trimmed to take the bunting iron. In making the hole, he pushed the awl first from one side, then the other, and not right on through. Then Dan passed the root through and cut the basswood binding just

ahead of where the new root was to go. As he worked, he would cut the basswood binding just before he reached the point with the new sewing.

The root was passed in a double-thong stitch to the top end of the gunwale, where it was anchored.

The gunwales at the prow ends were now ready for binding, but before they could be bound they had to be trimmed with the crooked knife. First Dan trimmed the tips of the gunwales so that they were all the same length, then he rounded the front edges. This was not done at the other end until the gunwales had been bound.

Dan cut away the gunwales with the jackknife to form a trough that went right around them so that the binding would be recessed when it was applied. Starting about 10 mm (³/₈ in.) past the tip of the end piece, he drew a line around the gunwales with a pencil, and 3 cm (1¹/₈ in.) forward of that, he drew another line around them. Then he made cuts along the lines with the jackknife and removed the wood to a depth of about 3 mm (¹/₈ in.) in effect producing a waist.

The binding was then started using a piece of spruce root 6 mm (¹/₄ in.) wide. Trapping the tip of it between the upper and lower outer gunwales just in front of the recess, he cut it with the jackknife. Dan wrapped the root

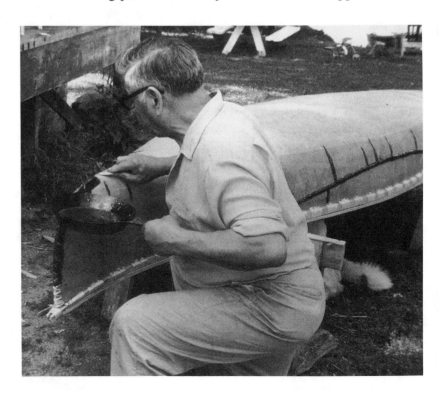

Inverted now, the canoe is sealed from the outside with spruce gum. Dan applies it with a cedar spatula. (Photo by Denis Alsford, National Museums of Canada.)

around and around the gunwales, gradually working toward the end piece, so that the last wrap passed through a hole made in the front edge of the end piece. He tied it off under the gunwales; then, using the crooked knife, he trimmed the leading tips of the gunwales to look neat.

At this point, the last ribs to have been put in Dan tapped home still further.

It was now time to gum the canoe. Dan tipped the canoe slightly onto one side using an odd length of cedar as a prop under the gunwale. Then he used the jackknife to trim the seam along the side of the canoe where the side pieces had been added to the main bark piece. Where the bark overlapped, the external edges had been left square; now he cut them so that they met the canoe at an angle.

Dan did not know how the gum had been prepared in the old days. He had tried experimenting by boiling the spruce gum in a pail of water, expecting the gum to stay at the bottom and the dirt to rise, but the opposite happened. He intended to try other methods sometime, but for now he strained the gum through a piece of sacking.

He prepared for the job by building a fire outside the workshop and burning off the old frying pan that he used for melting the gum. He wanted the pan clean, because the dirty residue left from last time would cause the gum to darken, and he liked it to be a light, natural color.

Next, he made a strainer for the gum, using a piece of an old flour sack about 45 cm (18 in.) square (he said he would prefer to use cheesecloth if he had it). This he laid on the bench, and then cut two pieces of cedar 20 cm (8 in.) by 4.5 cm ($1^3/4$ in.) by 16 mm ($5/8$ in.) and smoothed them somewhat with the crooked knife. He drove a 3.8-cm ($1^1/2$-in.) nail through one piece, so that when it was right through, he cut 13 mm ($1/2$ in.) off and hammered over the end across the width. Then he split the piece along its length down to the nail, which prevented the wood from splitting completely in two. The split was 6 mm ($1/4$ in.) long. This produced a rough peg. He did the same with the other piece of wood.

He folded the sacking into three along its length, pushed one end into the split in the peg, then nailed it in place. He followed the same procedure at the other end of the sacking with the second peg. Where the sacking overlapped in between the two pegs, he opened it up, thus creating a bag with a handle at each end.

The following morning he lit a fire in the stove, put a long bench seat in the middle of the workshop, and in the center of this placed the sacking bag. He produced some spruce gum from a large paper bag; this he put into the cleaned pan, and placed it on the stove to melt. At this time Dan's wife came in to help, and they sat down on the bench with the bag between them. Taking a handle each, they practiced twisting the bag in opposite directions so that they would not make a mistake when straining the spruce gum.

While they waited for the gum to melt, Dan fashioned a piece of cedar into a spatula 20 cm (8 in.) by 19 mm ($3/4$ in.) by 6 mm ($1/4$ in.). He smoothed and rounded the sides and ends.

When the gum was melted, Dan stirred it and lifted out pieces of debris floating on top. The sacking strainer was lying across another cleaned frying pan, and he poured the gum into this. Then Dan and his wife lifted the strainer, took an end each, and twisted in opposite directions, thus forcing the gum out through the sacking and allowing it to drip into the pan.

Once the straining had been done, Dan added some resin to the gum to make it set harder. He put the pan onto the stove and heated the mixture, stirring it with the spatula. He tested the gum on the spatula by dipping it into cold water and rubbing it with his finger. He decided it was too hard, so he added two teaspoonfuls of bear grease to the mixture, stirred it, and tested it again, this time by allowing the gum to drip off the spatula. It fell slowly, almost congealing as it fell, and Dan decided that it was about right.

He turned the canoe over again so that it rested on the prow tips, and tilted it to one side. Then he began the sealing process, starting at one prow.

With his frying pan of gum in one hand and his spatula in the other, he proceeded to ladle the gum out of the pan, taking as much as the spatula would hold on the last 19 mm ($3/4$ in.). This he applied to the prow seam, beginning at the bottom of the canoe. Then he wet a thumb in his mouth so that the gum would not stick to him and pressed the gum into

Golden Lake paddles. (Photo by Denis Alsford, National Museums of Canada.)

position until he was satisfied that it had gotten into the crack or around the spruce root binding. He then smoothed the edges in the same way.

He worked on a section, completing 10 to 12 cm (4 to 5 in.) at a time. After the first section of the prow, he decided that he was not satisfied with the gum's consistency, so he added another teaspoonful of bear grease, then a little more gum, while heating it on the stove. He tested it again and removed a small piece of debris. Then he resumed gumming.

After he had finished one side of one prow, he gummed the seams on that side of the canoe, working his way along from the completed prow until all the vertical seams and a small split had been gummed. Once he had completed the other prow on that side, he laid the canoe over on its other side, and beginning with the first prow, gummed the other side. At a couple of points during the process, he had to reheat the gum, which had begun to get cold and set.

When he had finished the gumming, he righted the canoe and put two scrap pieces of cedar under the bottom to raise the canoe so that the gummed seams would not touch the bed. He placed the pieces so that when the canoe was tilted they were between the seams that had just been gummed. Then, with the canoe tilted, he tied a string around the center thwart and secured it to the leg of the bench. This raised the side of the canoe so that the long seam along the side was high.

Dan reheated the gum once again, then started gumming this seam. The same procedure was followed for the other side, then Dan untied the canoe and laid it on the two prow tips again. He closely inspected the skin of the canoe for small splits. At points where he thought there might be a split, he put his mouth over the spot and sucked. If there indeed was a split, then he would feel a draft of air on his tongue and know it had to be sealed. Before applying the gum to these splits, however, he would first cut the edges of the split to form a V.

Dan next prepared a length of basswood binding (1.82 m or 6 ft.) and tied it along the center thwart to form two shallow loops, through which the blades of the paddles would pass. To stop the loops from slipping along the thwart, he tied them with one side around the

shoulder of the thwart. He drilled a pair of holes through the intermediate thwart at each side and looped a piece of basswood binding through each pair to hold the handle of the paddle.

Dan was not satisfied with the basswood at the center thwart, however, so he cut it off and decided to make the tie with a piece of deerskin instead. The deerskin was from a buck that Dan had shot about sixteen years previously, and he had been using it ever since for odd jobs, including making a pair of moccasins and numerous lengths of string.

The canoe was now completed, so the two of us lifted it off the bed and carried it outside. Dan then picked it up, hoisted it over his head, and lowered it down onto his shoulders so that the flat blades of the paddles rested on his shoulders. He carried it down past his house to the lake and put the canoe into the water. His wife joined him from the house and climbed into the canoe, sitting between the intermediate and center thwarts, with her back toward the prow at her end. Then Dan climbed in and knelt between the center thwart and the other intermediate thwart, facing his wife and the direction in which he paddled.

The canoe sat low in the water, so that the waterline was almost up to the side seams, only about 2.5 to 5 cm (1 to 2 in.) below it. Dan paddled around for about ten minutes, then returned to the landing stage, where they both disembarked. He then lifted the canoe from the water and carried it to the woodshed, where a pair of sawhorses were set up. He first put the canoe on the ground and inspected the inside to see if there were any signs of leaks. There appeared to be one small leak, so he turned the canoe over and set it up on the sawhorses for close inspection. He tested the skin here and there with the sucking method and turned up two small leaks. After warming the gum on the fire again, he used it to seal the splits. He then deemed the canoe fit and ready.

Daniel Sarazin tries out his finished canoe. (Photo by Denis Alsford, National Museums of Canada.)

Algonquin Canoe Terms

The following are words and expressions in Algonquin relating to the birchbark canoe. They come from various informants and published sources. The source or sources follow the definition of the terms.

The published sources are Cuoq (1886), Lemoine (1911), and McGregor (1987).

The informants, nearly all of whom were birchbark canoe builders, are Jocko Carle, River Désert Algonquin, Maniwaki, Québec; William Commanda, River Désert Algonquin, Maniwaki, Québec; Irene Jerome, Barrière Lake Algonquin, Rapid Lake, Québec; James Jerome, Barrière Lake Algonquin, Rapid Lake, Québec; Lina Nottaway, Barrière Lake Algonquin, Rapid Lake, Québec; John Ratt, Barrière Lake Algonquin, Rapid Lake, Québec; Dan Sarazin, Golden Lake Algonquin, Golden Lake, Ontario; Basil Smith, River Désert Algonquin, Maniwaki, Québec; and Pierre Wawatie, Barrière Lake Algonquin, Rapid Lake, Québec.

The vocabulary of the birchbark canoe is not possesed by every native Algonquin speaker, just as the average native English or French speaker may not recognize *thwart* and *gunwale cap* or *barre de travers* and *couvre-plat-bord*. A number of the terms included here are old and rarely if ever heard among the canoe builders.

Some words—*wâgina, pîmitasa, apisidagan,* and others—are so important that they take the animate form. As well, there are a few differences in the parts of the canoe between Algonquin bands. *Pîmitasa* is *thwart* in Maniwaki, and the Barrière Lake builders use the word *apikan*, to give one example.

The alert reader will notice, by referring to Baraga, that many of these words were known to the Ojibway canoe builders.

The following is a list of abbreviations used from the published sources:
abs. - absolu (intransitive)
dim. - diminutif (diminutive)

en comp. - en composition (in composition)
g. a. - genre animé (animate form)
g. in. - genre inanimé (inanimate form)
lit. - literally
n. an. - noun, animate
n. in. - noun, inanimate
plur. - pluriel (plural)
s. a. - sujet animé (animate subject)
s. in. - sujet inanimé (inanimate subject)
v. int. - verb, intransitive
v. tra. - verb, transitive

äbwi - short implement for propelling the canoe (Cuoq:10; Lemoine:82; McGregor:6; JC; WC; JJ; BS; DS)

äbwikâs-azo - to make oneself a paddle (Lemoine:82)

äbwikaw (g.a.) - to make a paddle for someone (Lemoine:82)

äbwike - to make a paddle (Lemoine:82; JC; WC)

äbwing - on the paddle (Lemoine:82)

äbwins - small paddle (Cuoq:10; Lemoine:82; JC; WC)

äbwisak - a. paddle wood, maple (Lemoine:82; Cuoq:10). b. maple, because one ordinarily uses this wood to make paddles. Paddles were also made of white birch, ash, spruce, cedar, or other wood, depending on the qualities desired in the paddle.

agatoatik - bow piece of cedar; same name as crooked stick to feel for beaver *waj* (JJ). The living canoe makers most often use *wâginawinj* for the stem-piece.

agohaneonatik - gunwale that goes on top (LN). The gunwale cap in Maniwaki is called *apatapihikâhigan.*

agwadagwadjigan - piece of bark added on side to augment main bark sheet (WC; BS)

agwätcönak - out of the canoe (Lemoine:106)

aiakom-o - to be in a canoe (if one is floating) (Cuoq:33; Lemoine:106)

akimâk - ash (Cuoq:32; McGregor:13; JC;

WC). Sometimes used for thwarts and paddles because it is strong but not brittle.

akokwadjiganeiap - binding (DS)

akom-o - to be in a canoe (Cuoq:33; Lemoine:106)

akomowewebinabi - to fish in a canoe (Cuoq:33; Lemoine:106)

amikwandak-kok (plur.) - white spruce (also means jackpine) (Cuoq:37; Lemoine:241)

amônakise - fall from the canoe (Cuoq:299; Lemoine:106)

anämönak - under the canoe (Cuoq:40,99; Lemoine:109; McGregor:32)

andokwam - to go look for bark (Cuoq:439; Lemoine:215)

anin endäsönagaking? - how many canoes are there? (Lemoine:106)

anin endasonakisiwatc? - how many canoes are there? (Cuoq:299; Lemoine:106)

anoki tîmân - hunting canoe, usually 14 feet (JC; WC; JJ)

anokodjawanatik - "stick from the front" (LN). In Maniwaki, this is the *wâginawinj*.

apatapikâhigan - gunwale cap (Lemoine:86; JC; WC; JJ)

apickamon - bark for the knees (in the canoe) (Lemoine:215). This seems to be an old word, as several informants did not recognize it.

apikan - thwart (JJ; LN). Most commonly, this word means tumpline. In Rapid Lake, it means any thwart of the canoe. In the canoe carry, the tumpline is attached to the center thwart. The River Désert and Golden Lake word for thwart is *pîmitasa*.

apikanenj - little thwart (LN)

apikotazowin - kind of hand-leather worn by those using a crooked knife (Cuoq:56). This word is probably unknown today. It may mean a glove or piece of leather that was worn on the hand using the crooked knife to avoid blisters.

apisidagan-ik (plur.) - sheathing or planking (Cuoq:58; McGregor:48; JC; WC; JJ; BS)

asanackat (v.int.) - same as *asani*, though *asani* specifies the tree, whereas *asanackat* specifies the bark (McGregor:437)

asani (v.int.) - birch bark adheres tightly to the tree; the bark cannot be peeled without tearing (McGregor:437)

aton-o - to make a canoe (Cuoq:69; Lemoine:106; McGregor:58; WC). This is the old verb for canoe making, still recog-

nized by most of the living canoe makers. The newer one, and the one most often used, is tcîmanike.

av-aho (en comp.) - to go by canoe (Lemoine:106)

awas inakäkeönak - on that side of the canoe (Lemoine:106)

awätahoj (g.a.) - to transport by canoe (Lemoine:106)

awätahotan (g.in.) - to transport by canoe (Lemoine:106)

awätahodjige (absolu) - to transport by canoe (Lemoine:106)

cangopiwidjik mitikok - spruce (DS)

cecekatik - black spruce (JJ)

cidakwahigan - wedge (JJ)

cikinum - whole assembly of putting up sides of a canoe and bark (BS)

cingop - spruce (Cuoq:91; DS) or balsam fir (McGregor:378)

cingwak - pine (Cuoq:91; McGregor:378)

gackikon-o - to lash a canoe (Lemoine:144; McGregor:84; DS). From this comes the noun form *gackikonowin*, the lacing on the gunwales.

gwaiakwa - straight; said often of bows that line up straight (BS)

inahodjige (absolu) - to take by canoe to a certain place; to take by canoe in a certain manner (Lemoine:106)

inahoj (g.a.) - to take by canoe to a certain place; to take by canoe in a certain manner (Lemoine:106)

inahotan (g.in.) - to take by canoe to a certain place; to take by canoe in a certain manner (Lemoine:106)

inav-aho - to go by canoe to a certain place; to go by canoe in a certain manner (Lemoine:106)

ineaik - finish end (DS)

ininackwai - good bark; canoe bark (Cuoq:128; Lemoine:215; McGregor:437; WC; DS). This is always darker on the outside than *waceckwai* (WC)

ininandag - balsam fir (Cuoq:128; McGregor:378)

i nisadjiwang inakak - downstream (Lemoine:80)

inokam - to be a certain number of people in a canoe (Cuoq:130; Lemoine:106) kackwemaginige (v.int.) - to scrape birch bark, as in adding designs (McGregor:437)

kapackweia (v.int.) - the bark is brittle or dry (McGregor:437)

kawandak-kok (plur.) - white spruce (Cuoq:150; Lemoine:241)

kijik-ak (plur.) - cedar (Cuoq: 159; Lemoine:109; McGregor:131; JC; WC; IJ; JJ; LN; BS; DS)

kîjîkika - there is cedar there (Cuoq:159; Lemoine:109)

kîjîkikang - the place where cedar grows (Cuoq:159; Lemoine:109)

kimoton-o (n.in.) - to steal a canoe (Cuoq:299; Lemoine:106)

kinabadjigan (n.in.) - anchor (McGregor:357)

kipijidawan - foot measure as measured by two lengths of the end of the thumb to the end of the little finger (JJ)

kiweh-o - to return by canoe (Cuoq:179)

kiwehodjige (absolu) - to bring back by canoe (Lemoine:106)

kîwehoj (g.a.) - to bring back by canoe (Cuoq:179; Lemoine:106)

kîwehotan (g.in.) - to bring back by canoe (Lemoine:106)

kîwekom-o - to return by canoe (Cuoq:33; Lemoine:106)

kokokabi (v.int.) - canoe is rocking (caused by water sloshing in canoe) (Cuoq:182; McGregor:151)

kokokase (v.int.) - the canoe rocks, teeters, see-saws (Cuoq:182; McGregor:151)

kokokwa (s.in.) - tippy (Cuoq:182; Lemoine; WC)

-kop (en comp.) - bark (Lemoine:215)

mackikwätik - red spruce (Cuoq:193; Lemoine:241); tamarack (McGregor:180)

mâdjahodjige (absolu) - to carry by canoe (Lemoine:106)

mâdjahoj (g.a.) - to carry by canoe (Lemoine:106)

mâdjahotan (g.in.) - to carry by canoe (Lemoine:106)

madjonenjic - worthless little canoe (Cuoq:299; Lemoine:106)

makade minahig (n.in.) - black spruce (McGregor:198)

mam-, ma- (en comp.) - downstream (Cuoq:200; Lemoine:80)

mâming - downstream (Cuoq:200; Lemoine:80)

mämiwinini, omâmiwinini - downriver man (Cuoq:200; Lemoine:80). This is the word for Algonquin in the Algonquin language.

manadabi (v.int.) - dig for spruce root (Cuoq:203; McGregor:414). This is a different word than is used for the actual preparation of spruce root.

mänatâpaning - place where one obtains spruce root (Cuoq:203; Lemoine: "watap")

mâneokamok - there are several people in a canoe (Lemoine:106)

manikop-i - to harvest little bark (Lemoine:215)

manikwam - to harvest bark (Cuoq:205; Lemoine:215; McGregor:178,230,437)

maninagekobinan (v.tra.) - peel the bark from a tree (McGregor:418)

masinatan - decoration (JJ)

mätaton-o - to take the canoe to water (Lemoine:106)

miciwatikowikwas - old birch tree with bark that is worth nothing (Cuoq:439)

mijagamekwajiwe (v.int.) - arrive by paddling (McGregor:193)

mijaka-ke - to arrive by canoe (Cuoq:218; Lemoine:106; McGregor:194)

mijakickam (v.int.) - arrive by stepping out of canoe into shallow water (Cuoq:218; McGregor:193)

mijakihige (v.int.) - arrive by poling or pushing with a paddle in shallow water (McGregor:193)

mîkos - awl (Cuoq:217; McGregor:193; JC; WC; JJ; BS; DS)

minahik-ikok (plur.) - white spruce (Lemoine:241; JJ); spruce (McGregor:198,378)

minaik - red pine. The gum of the red pine is the best for gumming canoes. (Cuoq:224). Some Indian canoe builders would disagree with Cuoq.

miskwa wîkwâs - red birch bark (WC). This is a reddish sort of bark from the white birch; generally too dry for use as canoe bark.

miskwawâk - red cedar (Cuoq:231; Lemoine:109)

mitikötcîmân - wooden canoe (Lemoine:106)

mitikötcitahaskwan - wooden peg (JC; WC). These pegs are hardwood and are either round or square. They are put horizontally through the inwale and outwale and down through the gunwale cap into the gunwale.

mitik sakakwegan - wooden peg (JJ)

mitjimakwahiganan - stake (JJ)

mokomân - knife (Cuoq:238; Lemoine:148; McGregor:212; JC; WC; JJ; BS; DS)

mokotâgan (g.a.) - crooked knife (Cuoq:239; Lemoine:148; McGregor:212; JC; WC; JJ; BS)

mokotaganak - crooked knife handle (Cuoq:239)

monanadabi (v.int.) - dig for spruce root (McGregor:414)

mose pïkew - soft gum with worms in it (BS)

nadawa-e (v.tra.) - approach by canoe; fetch by canoe (McGregor:219)

nadawikwase - look for bark (JJ)

nadjibiam - to go by canoe to fetch drink (Cuoq:247)

najonikek tcîmân - two-fathom canoe (Lemoine:106)

nanda mänatäpi - to go harvest root (Lemoine)

nandohikiwe - to go harvest gum (Lemoine:292)

nandokwam - to go look for bark (Lemoine:215; McGregor:230,437; JC; WC)

nandawanakekwe - to go harvest large sheets of bark (Cuoq:257)

napaki tcîmân - flat canoe, boat (Lemoine:106)

nâton-o - to go look for a canoe (Cuoq:263,299; Lemoine:106)

nesonikek tcîmân - three-fathom canoe (Lemoine:106)

newäpinan tcîmân - canoe of four places (Lemoine:106)

nibaham (v.int.) - to canoe or travel by night (Cuoq:280; McGregor:405)

nictäna täsônak - twenty canoes (Lemoine:106)

nictäna täsônakisiwäk - there are twenty canoes (Lemoine:106)

nîjokamok - they are two in a canoe (Cuoq:130; Lemoine:106)

nîjônagaton - there are two canoes (Cuoq:299; Lemoine:106)

nîjônak - two canoes (Cuoq:271; Lemoine:106)

nijonik - two units of measure constituting two arms' lengths (Cuoq:272; PW)

nîkanav-aho - to go ahead by canoe (Cuoq:273; Lemoine:106)

nîkan inakâkeônak - ahead of the canoe (Lemoine:106)

nimitamaham - to go ahead by canoe if one is paddling (Cuoq:276; Lemoine:106)

nimitamahamowinini - bow man (Cuoq:276)

nimitamônak - bow of a canoe (Cuoq:276; Lemoine:106; McGregor:256)

ningâsimon-nan (plur.) - sail for boat or canoe (Lemoine)

ningasimo tcîmân - canvas canoe (Lemone:106; JJ). This is a wood-and-canvas canoe.

ningot äpinan tcîmân - canoe with a single place (Lemoine:106)

ningotönagat - there is one canoe (Cuoq:299; Lemoine:106)

ningotônak - one canoe (Lemoine:106)

ningotonakisiwak - they (the travelers) are in a single canoe (Lemoine:106)

nisokam - to be three in a canoe (Cuoq:282)

nisonakisiwak - there are three canoes (Cuoq:299)

nitamonak - prow (DS)

nitaojiwe - to ascend a rapids (Cuoq:283)

nockadjigan - strainer (Cuoq:284)

nockandjikawidjigan - strainer (DS)

nokackweia (v.int.) - birch bark is soft and pliable (Cuoq:285; McGregor:267)

odakan (n.in.) - stern of a canoe (Cuoq:310; McGregor:273)

odapabigibidjige (v.int.) - pull a canoe or boat up rapids (McGregor:274)

odjipik - root (McGregor:277; DS). This is a general word for root, not as precise as *watap*.

ogickiwe - get cedar (JJ)

ojit - 6 feet as measured by two arms' lengths (JJ)

okasipimite - walleye grease (used by Patrick Maranda to mix with spruce gum to gum canoe) (LN)

okidjahi mitik - sapwood (JJ)

okikens - red pine (McGregor:378)

okiwe - get gum (JJ)

-ön (en comp.) - canoe (Cuoq:299; Lemoine:106)

onackweia (v.int.) - the birch bark is smooth (McGregor:437)

-ônägät - the canoe is (such and such) (Lemoine:106)

onagek (n.an.) - bark of a tree (McGregor:418)

-önak (en comp.) - canoe (Cuoq:299; Lemoine:106)

onakodjiawonakwatik - headboard (JJ). The headboard in River Désert is called *otinimanganikadjigan*.

onakomakahigan - building bed (JJ)

onakwadjonagwatik - stem-piece (JJ). The River Désert word for stem-piece is *wåkinawinj*.

ondas inakâkeönak - on this side of the canoe (Cuoq:299; Lemoine:106)

onedeckodjigan - building frame (DS)

onitehgan - building frame (JJ)

otäbwie - to make a paddle stroke (Lemoine:82)

otäbwin - to make a paddle of something (Lemoine:82)

otâkan - stern of a canoe (Cuoq:310; Lemoine:106)

otâke - to take by canoe (being in the stern) (Cuoq:310; Lemoine:106)

otcîmân-i - to have a canoe (Lemoine:106)

otehmitik - heartwood (JJ)

otijak - lenticels, or eyes, of bark (JJ)

otinimanganikadjigan - headboard; literally, "shoulder device" (WC)

pakahajigwe (v.int.) - remove bark (especially birch bark) from trees (McGregor:178)

pakamâgan - hammer (Lemoine; DS)

pakitehigan - hammer (Cuoq:323; Lemoine)

pakojidan - side piece (JJ)

pakwaajikwanak - instrument which helps to remove bark from birches for canoe construction (Cuoq:324)

pakwahajikwe (absolu) - to remove bark from a tree (Cuoq:324; Lemoine:215: McGregor:230,437)

pakwahôn-o - to patch a canoe (Cuoq:325; Lemoine:106)

pakwani (v.int.) - bark is removable; denotes time of year when bark is easily peeled from tree (McGregor:230,418,437)

pakwaon-o - to repair a canoe (Cuoq:325)

pakweciman - bark for knees (JJ). Possibly the same as *apickamon.*

panipisakahigan - bone chisel (DS). A chisel is often used for making a mortise in the inwale to receive the thwart.

papackikiw - balsam gum (Lemoine; McGregor:316,378; DS)

papackiw - balsam gum (McGregor:316,378)

papogonan wikwas - take off bark (JJ)

pasâbikahigan - the cedars, a place (Lemoine:109)

pasahan (v.tra.) - fetching or obtaining cedar for canoe splints or pelt stretchers (McGregor:318)

pasahiganing - stand of cedars; lit., where one goes to obtain cedar for canoe making (McGregor:131,317)

pasahige - a. to go look for cedar (for ribs, etc.) (Lemoine:109; McGregor:317); b. to split cedar for ribs (Lemoine)

pasahitabane - to split cedar for ribs (Lemoine)

pejikokam - there is only one canoe (Cuoq:130; Lemoine:106)

pejikokam - to be alone in a canoe (Cuoq:332; Lemoine:106)

pëtäbwie - to paddle slowly (Lemoine)

picaganadabi (v.int.) - peel spruce root, or scrape off the exterior cover or membrane (McGregor:414)

pïcakikibij (g.a.) - to take off bark (Lemoine:215)

pïcakikibiton (g.in.) - to take off bark (Lemoine:215)

picanakekwe - to take off the bark from a birch tree (Cuoq:334)

pî inahodjige (absolu) - to bring by canoe (Lemoine:106)

pî inahoj (g.a.) - to bring by canoe (Lemoine:106)

pî inahotan (g.in.) - to bring by canoe (Lemoine:106)

pikikanatik - spatula (used for scraping the spruce gum and grease mixture) (JJ)

pïkikâtan-kaj (g.a.) - to gum (Lemoine:292)

pïkikäzo (s.a.), pïkikäzo-kate (s.in.) - it is gummed (Lemoine:292)

pïkike - to gum (Cuoq:336; Lemoine:292)

pikiwewan pikiw - resin (DS)

pïkiw (g.a.), pïkiw-wens (dim.) - gum (Cuoq:336; Lemoine:292; JC; WC; JJ; BS; DS)

pî kîwehodjige (absolu) - to bring back by canoe (Lemoine:106)

pî kîwehoj (g.a.) - to bring back by canoe (Lemoine:106)

pî kîwehotan (g.in.) - to bring back by canoe (Lemoine:106)

pïkiwewan - gum (on trees) (Lemoine:292)

pikwakokan - peg (DS)

pïmâciwagan - sail of boat or canoe (Lemoine)

pïmicka - to paddle (Lemoine:82)

pimikwan-ak (plur.) - gunwale (JC; WC; JJ; BS). This can mean inwale, outwale, or both together.

pimikwanatik - gunwale (JJ). This is the same word as above, simply with the addition of a suffix meaning wood.

piminikwan - string (DS)

pîmitasa - thwart (Cuoq:340; Lemoine:86; JC; WC; BS; DS)

pîmitasake - to make a thwart (Cuoq:340; Lemoine:86)

pimite - grease (Cuoq:340; Lemoine:294; JC; WC; JJ; BS; DS). Mixed with resin from a coniferous tree, this can be bear grease, commercial lard or even, as in the case of Patrick Maranda's usage, walleye grease.

pîndakinawe - to put the ribs in the canoe (Cuoq:342; Lemoine)

pindônak - in the canoe (Cuoq:342; Lemoine:106)

pipakickweia wîkwâs - paper birch (JJ). The meaning here is that the bark is "papery" and delaminates too easily, and therefore is not good for canoe making. In apposition to this, "canoe birch" would mean that the bark is good for canoe making.

pipakiwaian tcîmân - canvas canoe (Lemoine:106)

pipon wîkwâs - winter bark (JC; WC; JJ).

pîtahodjige (absolu) - to bring by canoe (Lemoine:106)

pîtahoj (g.a.) - to bring by canoe (Lemoine:106)

pîtahotan (g.in.) - to bring by canoe (Lemoine:106)

pîtc inahodjige (absolu) - to bring by canoe (Lemoine:106)

pîtc inahoj (g.a.) - to bring by canoe (Lemoine:106)

pîtc inahotan (g.in.) - to bring by canoe (Lemoine:106)

pitobiton (g.in.) - to take bark off (Lemoine:215)

pitockwai (n.in.) - bark of the gray birch, a variety of white birch whose bark does not lend itself to canoe building (McGregor:437); bark of inferior quality that separates in layers (WC).

pitockwan - layered bark that separates (JJ)

piwikotagan - shavings made by a crooked knfie, as differentiated from shavings made with another kind of tool (Cuoq:337,351; McGregor:352)

pokogan - birchbark structure built to provide shelter for the canoe building bed (JR)

pokojidan - side piece (JJ)

pokonêcin - tear one's canoe (Lemoine:106); Cuoq (353) defines this as wrecking the canoe, but then a note by Thavenet says that this is perhaps too strong a word, but he does not know another way to express well the fact that the canoe was pushed into a rock by the current, and that a piece of bark was torn.

ponisasowin - anchor (Cuoq:353; McGregor:357)

pôs-i - to depart by canoe (Cuoq:354; Lemoine:106)

pôsitas-o - to load one's canoe (Lemoine:106; McGregor:357)

rabeska - old-style Algonquin canoe, or fur trade canoe (JC; WC). Adney (1964:122) says that the Algonquin called the large fur trade canoes *nabiska* (there's no "r" in the language) and that the Têtes de Boule Indians used the word *rabeska*. All living informants recognize this word and its definition, though it does not seem to be an Algonquin term.

sakahagan - stake (McGregor:362; DS). This refers to either an inner or outer stake in canoe construction.

sakikisi (s.a.) - it splits badly (Lemoine:266; McGregor:361)

sesekandak-kok (plur.) - a. black spurce (Lemoine:241; McGreogr:198,365,378); b. white spruce (Cuoq:366)

sintakwahiganatikok - This word, which is in the plural here, means battens of wood that perform the function of the binder (BS)

tackanadabi (v.int.) - split spruce for stitching material (McGregor:414)

tackigwan (n.in.) - birch bark that has been removed from a tree by slitting to the desired length (McGregor:437)

tackikahigan - wedge (Cuoq:377; Lemoine:124; DS). This is the wedge used to split wood.

tackikaisan - wood split in two (Lemoine). One of the many illustrations in this list of the marvels of the Algonquin verb. This description isn't formed as in English or French (*bois fendu en deux*), but rather a completely new verb is formed from familiar roots.

takonakise - the canoes approach each other

(Lemoine:106)

takwahoton-o - to put the ribs in the canoe (Lemoine)

tanagan - wedge (Cuoq:384; Lemoine:124; McGregor:394; BS; DS). A wedge used for splitting wood or to raise the bow to form the rocker as the canoe is being set up.

tangônak - along both sides (Cuoq:382; Lemone:106)

tatojan-jv (g.a.) - to split the long way (Lemoine:266)

tatojige (absolu) - to split the long way (Lemoine:266)

tcametc - canoeist (Cuoq:391; Lemoine:106; McGregor:71)

tcigakodjigan - gore (JJ)

tcihicon-no - a. to trim the bark of a canoe under construction (Lemoine:215). b. "to trim the bark used for making a canoe. A technical term that expresses the action of trimming the bark that exceeds the height that one wants for the canoe"(Cuoq:390). c. "One of those working on a canoe, having finished what he was asked to do, asked what he was to do next: *Anin dac*, he said, *ket inanokiiân? Ki ga tciicon*, the boss answered him; you will trim the excess bark."

tcîmân - canoe (Cuoq:390; Lemoine:106; McGregor:70; JC; WC; IJ; JJ; LN; BS; DS; PW)

tcîmân abitaotôn - to paddle a canoe half the time (Lemoine:106)

tcîmânens (dim.) - little canoe (Lemoine:106; JC; WS; BS)

tcîmânijikwai (n.in.) - canoe bark (McGregor:437)

tcîmânike - to make a canoe (Lemone:106; McGregor:71; JC; WC; JJ; BS). This is the newer, more common, word for making a canoe. The old term is *aton-o*.

tcîmân mikos - large awl for making canoes of birch bark (Cuoq:217). A number of informants recall these being made with a bone blade and wooden handle.

tcîmân wîkwâs - canoe birch (JJ). Bark that is appropriate for canoe making, as opposed to bark that would be used for other things.

tcîme - to paddle (Cuoq:391; Lemoine:82; McGregor:72)

tcîmewinini - canoeist (Lemoine:106; McGregor:71)

tcitahaskwan - nail (Cuoq:393; McGregor:74; JC; WC; BS; DS)

tebigwam - to have enough bark (Lemoine:215; McGregor:437)

te ônagat - the canoe is large enough (Lemoine:106)

teswekakwahigan - binder (JJ)

tibakonan - double arm measure (LN)

tidibigwan (n.in.) - a rolled-up bundle of birch bark (McGregor:437)

tipahigans (dim.) - measuring stick (McGregor:403; JC; WC; JJ; DS)

tipaônan - canoe measure (Cuoq:402; Lemoine:106). It is possible that this is an older, more exact word for canoe measure, as *tipahigan* is quite general. The latter, however, is in more common use today among the canoe makers.

titibinagan - roll of bark (Cuoq:403; Lemoine:215; McGregor:407,437)

wâbanäki tcîmân - new-style canoe; Abnaki canoe (JC; WC). This style, virtually the only style made today, was adopted by the Algonquin at the turn of the century.

wabidjidab-i (v.int.) - to load, as a vehicle or a canoe (McGregor:357)

waceckwai - white, shiny, or paper birch, good for a canoe (WC)

wâgina-nak (plur.) - rib of canoe (Cuoq:416; Lemoine; McGregor:416; JC; WC)

wâginagan - red spruce (Lemoine:241)

waginakwe - put ribs in (McGregor:416; JJ)

waginatik - rib (JJ)

wâginawinj - stem-piece (Cuoq:416; Lemoine; McGregor:416; JC; WC)

waiekwa - end of canoe (DS)

wakakwat - ax (Lemoine:300)

wäkitônak - on the canoe (Cuoq:419; Lemoine:109)

wanakek - bark (McGregor:418; DS). This term denotes bark in general. Birch bark is *wîkwâs.*

wanakodjaônak - prow of the canoe (Cuoq:422; Lemoine:106; McGregor:419; DS)

wanihige tcîmân - trapping canoe, often 10 or 12 feet long (JC; WC)

watap-pik (plur.) - red spruce root for lashing (Cuoq:426; Lemoine; McGregor:414; JC; JJ). Cuoq says that the word is so frequently used in French in Canada that it merits adoption by the French Academy.

watapi - to get spruce root (JJ)

watapicak (vitupératif) - old spruce root (Lemoine:241)

webäsôno - the canoe is taken by the wind (Lemoine:106)

wibônagat - the canoe is narrow (Lemoine:106)

wîbônak - a narrow canoe (Cuoq:434; Lemoine:106)

wikopiminj - basswood (Cuoq:438; Lemoine:93; McGregor:436; DS). The inner bark of the basswood is often used in birchbark canoe construction as a cord for tying.

wîkwâs - birch; birch bark (Cuoq:439; Lemoine:97,215; McGregor:437; JC; WC; IJ; JJ; LN; JR; BS; DS; PW)

wikwasiwi - birch (DS)

wîkwâs tcîmân - birchbark canoe (Cuoq:391; Lemoine:215; McGregor:70; JC; WC; IJ; JJ; LN; JR; BS; DS; PW)

wisakedjak - moss on canoe birch (JJ). According to Jim Jerome, this moss, different from sphagnum moss, tends to grow on good-quality bark.

Glossary

abaft - nearer stern, aft of.

amidships - in the middle of the canoe.

athwartships - from side to side.

back stitch - stitch in which the root doubles back each time on the preceding stitch.

balk - roughly squared wood beam.

batten - long, narrow strip of wood.

beam - canoe's breadth.

bellied - usually used to describe a headboard that is bent permanently out toward the stem-piece.

bevel - cut at an angle.

bilge - where canoe bottom and side meet.

binder - batten assembly that is braced to form the ribs while they are drying in the canoe.

bitter end - last extremity.

broken rib - a rib near the bow that is broken to conform to a sharp centerline.

building bed - ground on which the canoe is staked out and constructed.

building frame - gunwalelike assembly used for forming the bottom of the canoe. May be a formed sheet of plywood.

building platform - a building bed of boards rather than dirt.

bulkhead - partition separating parts of the canoe; in a birchbark canoe, the headboard.

camber - upward curve or convexity.

carving horse - bench on which the worker sits, having an arm to clamp wood for carving or shaving. Also called a shaving horse.

centerline - imaginary line from bow to bow along the center of the canoe.

chin - profile in the bow created by tumblehome.

chine - an angular intersection of the sides and bottom of a canoe.

clamped - used to describe sheathing that is pressed or held into place, as in a birchbark canoe, as opposed to being fastened into place.

close-wrapped - wrapped continuously, as in wrapping of a stem-piece with basswood bark.

cover - bark sheet.

crossbar - thwart.

cross-stitch - stitch where diagonal roots cross each other in the middle at right angles.

crowned - used to describe a building bed raised in the middle.

cutwater - outer surface of the bow, which meets the water.

deck-piece - transversal piece of bark at the bow that usually goes over the inwales and down the sides. Sometimes simply called a flap.

double-thong stitch - stitch where each length of root goes through the same hole, but from opposite sides.

edge-to-edge - usually used to describe positioning of gores with a V taken out so that the edges can be sewn together rather than overlapped. Also used for sheathing laid with the edges together rather than overlapped.

elevation - refers to thickness, for example, when describing a thwart in plan view.

fair - make smooth and regular.

feathered - used to describe butts of sheathing that overlap one inside the other.

flap - of the pieces of birch bark in a canoe that are ordinarily described as flaps, the two most common are the ones used as deck-pieces and doubling pieces fitted along the gunwales mostly as decorations.

flare - widen gradually, usually in an upward direction.

former - term used by Denis Alsford for building frame.

forefoot - bottom of stem profile.

frames - another term for ribs.

framing - formation of the bows.

froe - tool used to split wood, having a horizontal blade and a vertical handle rising from it.

frog - small wood batten sometimes used to support the heel of the stem-piece.

gore - vertical slash made in the bark sheet to keep the sides from crimping.

gum - resin from trees, especially spruce, used to seal seams of a canoe. The term is also very loosely applied to tar.

gunwale - main longitudinal member of the canoe; the upper edge of its side.

headboard - vertical support of the bow, usually resting on the heel of the stem-piece and extending up to support the inwale.

heel - bottom end of the stem-piece.

hogged bottom - canoe bottom that is higher amidships than at the bows.

hogged sheer - a gunwale line that is higher in profile at the center thwart than at the intermediate thwarts.

inboard - toward the center of the canoe.

inwale - inner gunwale; sometimes called the main gunwale.

knuckle - slight protrusion on a profile line, sometimes on the forefoot of the stem-piece.

lacing - joining of sheets of bark or wooden member by passing root thong through holes and around the pieces to be joined.

lamina - one of several strips in a cedar batten, split and then bent to form the stem-piece.

lashing - the series of over-and-over stitches used to fix the bark sheet to the gunwales or to join bark sheets or wooden members to one another. Also called sewing or stitching.

lathing - see sheathing.

lining - term used by Denis Alsford for sheathing.

longitudinal - from one bow in the direction of the other.

manboard - headboard. This term is perhaps more commonly used with fur trade canoes, as this vertical bow member often had a little man painted on it.

maul - heavy wooden hammer.

midsection - center part of the canoe.

open spiral - a binding of the stem-piece, especially where the binding material is separated by intervals.

outboard - away from the center of the canoe.

outwale - a longitudinal member of the gunwale outboard of the bark.

panel - a piece of bark that is joined to the main bark to augment its width.

pay - smear with tar or gum.

peak - juncture of the gunwale and the stem head.

pinched in - describes gunwale outline that, when seen in plan view, first follows inwale line and then curves out to the stem-piece.

planking - see sheathing.

profile - side view or vertical cross section.

prow - the bow.

rabbet - a step-shaped channel sometimes cut on the face of the stem-piece inboard of the cutwater line to receive the end of the bark sheet.

rabeska - large fur trade canoe. Now often used by the Algonquin in western Québec to refer to the old-style Algonquin canoe.

rail cap - gunwale cap.

rake - sweep along or away from.

rib - transversal member that supports a canoe's structure on the interior surface of the hull.

rocker - in profile, the bottom longitudinal line of a canoe.

scraper - an implement used to abrade.

seam - juncture of bark sheets.

sewing - see lashing.

shaving horse - see carving horse.

sheathing - strakes that line the bottom of the canoe longitudinally between the bark and the ribs. Also called lathing or planking.

sheer - in profile, the top longitudinal line of a canoe.

shoulder - transversal cut near the end of the center thwart; transversal cut near the top of the headboard that supports the inwale.

slash - same as gore.

spiral stitch - stitch that goes form one side of the bark to the other, creating a spiral as it advances.

splint - piece of sheathing.

steaming box - box of wood or metal used to heat ribs for bending.

stem - bow or bow-piece of a canoe.

stem-band - batten placed over the ends of the bark at the stem to protect the seam of the bow.

stem head - top of stem-piece.

stem-piece - curved bow member that forms the bow profile, usually cedar.

stepped - placed or fitted on top of.

stitching - see lashing.

stop know - knot tied in the end of a root thong to keep it from going through a hole when beginning stitching.

strake - individual pieces of sheathing.

stressed - used to describe a rib that is held in place by pressure, as in a birchbark canoe.

strut - brace.

temporary rib - wooden member bent like a permanent canoe rib and put in place in the canoe to hold the sheathing in place so that the permanent ribs can be fitted.

thong - a strip, usually of root.

thwart - transversal member of the gunwale assembly.

topside - upper part, usually of canoe sides.

trim - adjustment of the balance of a canoe by distribution of weight.

tumblehome - incurving of upper sides of a canoe.

tumpline - strap that fits over forehead, used in canoe carry.

wall-sided - used to describe canoe with vertical sides.

waterline - on a canoe, the upper extent of the water when the canoe is in use.

wedge - V-shaped piece of wood.

wulegessis - deck-piece or flap. The word doesn't seem to have been used among the Algonquin.

Bibliography

Adney, Edwin Tappan. Notes. The Mariners' Museum, Newport News, Virginia.

Adney, Edwin Tappan, and Howard I. Chapelle. *The Bark Canoes and Skin Boats of North America.* Museums of History and Technology, Bulletin 230. Washington, D.C.: Smithsonian Institution, 1964.

"Aiamie-Tipadjimowin Masinaigan." Montréal, Québec: J. M. Valois, 1890.

Alcock, F. J. "The Long Sault of the Ottawa." *Canadian Geographic Journal* 45; no. 6 (December 1952): 252–61.

André, Louis. "Dictionnaire Algonquin." Manuscript. Oka, Québec, 1688(?).

———. "Préceptes, phrases et mots de la langue Algonquine Outaouaise pour un missionnaire nouveau." Manuscript. Archives des Jésuites à Montréal, Québec, 1688–1715.

Aubin, George. *Ethnographic Notes from Golden Lake.* Papers of the Thirteenth Algonquian Conference, 47–52. Ottawa, Ontario: Carleton University, 1982.

———. *Golden Lake Algonquin: Preliminary Report.* Papers of the Tenth Algonquian Conference, 121–25. Ottawa, Ontario: Carleton University, 1979.

———. *A Proto-Algonquian Dictionary.* Mercury Series, Canadian Ethnology Service, Paper no. 29. Ottawa, Ontario: National Museum of Man, 1976.

Beck, H. P. "Algonquin Folklore from Maniwaki." *Journal of American Folklore* 60 (1947): 259–64.

Belcourt, G. A. "Mon Itinéraire du Lac des Deux-Montagnes à la Rivière-Rouge." *Bulletin de la Société Historique de Saint-Boniface* 4 (1915).

Black, Meredith Jean. *Algonquin Ethnobotany: An Interpretation of Aboriginal Adaptation in Southwestern Québec.* Mercury Series, Canadian Ethnology Service, Paper no. 65. Ottawa, Ontario. National Museum of Man, 1980.

Bloomfield, Leonard. "Algonquian." In *Linguistic Structures of Native America*, 85–129. Viking Publications in Anthropology, No. 6. New York, 1946.

———. On the Sound System of Central Algonquian Language 1 (1925): 130–56.

Bond, C. C. J. "The Hudson's Bay Company in the Ottawa Valley." *The Beaver* 296 (1966): 4–21.

Brouillard, Edmond, and Marie Dumont-Anichinapeo. *Grammaire algonquine respectant les règles langagières coutumières propres aux communautés du Lac Simon ainsi que du Grand Lac Victoria.* Bande algonquine du Lac Simon, Lac Simon, Québec, 1987.

Building an Algonquin Birchbark Canoe. Greenville, New Hampshire: Trust for Native American Cultures and Crafts, 1984. Video, 52 min.

Canada Department of Forestry. *Native Trees of Canada.* 6th ed. Bulletin 61. Ottawa, Ontario, 1961.

Canada Department of Indian Affairs and Northern Development, Indian Affairs Branch. *Linguistic and Cultural Affiliations of Canadian Indian Bands.* Ottawa, Ontario: Queen's Printer, 1965.

Carrière, Gaston. *Un Grand Voltigeur: Le père Jean-Pierre Guéguen, O.M.I.* Guérin, Québec: Éditions de la Société historique Rivière des Quinze, 1978.

———. *Histoire documentaire de la Congrégation des Missionnaires Oblats de Marie-Immaculée dans l'Est du Canada.* Ottawa, Ontario: University of Ottawa, 1957–1970.

———. *Missionnaire sans toit: Le père Jean-Nicholas Laverlochère, O.M.I.* Montréal, Québec: Editions Rayonnement, 1963.

———. "Les Missions Catholiques dans l'Est du Canada et l'Honorable Compagnie de la Baie d'Hudson (1844–1900)." *Revue de l'Université d'Ottawa* 27, no. 1 (1957).

———. *Le Voyageur du Bon Dieu: Le père Jean-Marie Nédelec, O.M.I.* (1834–1896), 1961.

Cartier, Jacques. *The Voyages of Jacques Cartier.* Canadian Archivist Publications, no. 11. Translated by H. P. Bigger. 1914. Reprint. Ottawa, Ontario: F. A. Arcand, 1924.

Champlain, Samuel de. *Les Voyages de la nouvelle France.* Paris: C. Collet, 1632.

Chénier, Augustin. *Notes historiques sur le Témiscamingue.* Ville-Marie, Québec: Société d'histoire du Témiscamingue, 1937. Reprint 1980.

Couture, Y. H. *Les Algonquins.* Val d'Or, Québec: Éditions Hyperborée, 1983.

Cuoq, Jean-André. *Anotc Kekon.* Proceedings and Transactions of the Royal Society of Canada for the year 1894, vol. 11, no. 1: 137–79. Toronto, Ontario, Royal Society 1894.

———. *Cantique en langue algonquine.* Paris: Jouaust, 1872.

———. *Grammaire de la langue algonquine.* Mémoires de la Société Royale du Canada, Section I. 1891.

———. *Lexique de la langue algonquine.* Montréal, Québec: J. Chapleau et fils, 1886.

Davidson, D. S. *The Family Hunting Territories of the Grand Lac Victoria Indians.* Proceedings of the 22d International Congress of Americanists, no. 2: 69–95. Rome, 1926.

———. "Folk Tales from Grand Lake Victoria, Québec." *Journal of American Folklore* 41 (1928): 60.

Day, Gordon M. "The Name 'Algonquin.'" *International Journal of American Linguistics* 38, no. 4 (1972): 226–28.

Day, G., and Bruce Trigger. "Algonquin" In *Handbook of North American Indians: Northeast,* Washington, D.C.: Smithsonian Institution, 787–91. 1978.

Decontie, Pauline. *Kitiganzibi Anishnabeg.* Maniwaki, Québec: River Désert Band Council, 1974.

DS Productions, *Le dernier des Algonquins.* Paris: Video, 52 min. 1989.

Deschamps, Hubert. "Les Voyages de Samuel Champlain." In *Colonies et Empires.* Paris: Presses universitaires de France, 1951.

"Dictionnaire Algonquin-Français de l'an 1661." Oka, Québec, 1661.

"Dictionnaire Français-Algonquin." Manuscript. Oka, Québec, 1662(?).

"Dictionnaire Français-Algonquin." Manuscript. Oka, Québec, 1669.

Franquet, Louis. *Voyages et mémoires sur le Canada (1752).* Annuaire de l'Institut Canadien de Québec, 29–240. Québec: A. Côté, 1889.

Gidmark, David. *The Algonquin Birchbark Canoe.* Aylesbury, England: Shire Publications, 1988.

———. *Algonquin Birchbark Canoe Construction: A Preliminary Report.* Papers of the Sixteenth Algonquian Conference, Ottawa, Ontario: Carleton University, 1985.

———. *Birchbark Canoe.* Burnstown, Ontario: General Store Publishing House, 1989.

———. *The Birchbark Canoe Makers from the Barrière.* Papers of the Nineteenth Algonquian Conference, Ottawa, Ontario: Carleton University, 1988.

———. "Le canot d'écorce: quand la construction devient un art." *Expédition* (May–June 1987): 37–38.

———. "Ces canots d'écorce d'antan." *Sentier Chasse-Pêche* (April 1987): 38–42.

———. "Ethnographic Notes from Fieldwork among the Algonquin of Western Québec and Eastern Ontario." Manuscript and photographs. Gidmark, Maniwaki, Québec.

———. "Indian Birchbark Canoe Makers from Québec: Part I: William Commanda." *Wooden Canoe,* no. 30 (1987).

———. "Indian Birchbark Canoe Makers from Québec: Part II: Jocko Carle." *Wooden Canoe,* no. 34 (1988): 6–16.

———. "Indian Birchbark Canoe Makers from Québec: Part III: Jim Jerome." *Wooden Canoe,* no. 11 (1990): 8–16.

———. *The Indian Crafts of William and Mary Commanda.* Toronto, Ontario: McGraw-Hill Ryerson, 1980.

———. "Näverkanotbyggande: konst i utdöende." ("Birchbark canoe building: a dying art.") *Örnsköldsviks* (Sweden) Allehanda (July 18, 1985): 12.

———. "The Noble Canoe." *Reader's Digest* 116 (1980): 161–68.

Gillies, D. A. "Canot du Maître or Montréal Canoe." *Canadian Geographic Journal* 56 (1958): 3.

Gilstrap, Roger. *Algonquin dialect relationships in northwestern Québec.* Mercury Series, Canadian Ethnology Service, Paper no. 44. Ottawa, Ontario: National Museum of Man, 1978.

Gourd, Benoît-B. *Bibliographie de l'Abitibi-Témiscamingue.* Rouyn, Québec: Université du Québec en Abitibi-Témiscamingue, 1973.

Hansen, Keld. *Tjiman: en barkkano fra Canada* (Tcîmân: a bark canoe from Canada). Copenhagen: Mallings, 1981.

Hansen, Keld, and Jan Skamby Madsen. *Barkbåde* (Bark boat). Roskilde, Denmark: Viking-eskibshallen, 1981.

Hessel, Peter. "The Algonkins of Golden Lake." *The Beaver* (Winter 1983): 52–57.

———. *The Algonkin Tribe.* Arnprior, Ontario: Kitchesippi Books, 1987.

Henry, Alexander. *Travels and Adventures in Canada and in the Indian Territories between the Years 1760 and 1776.* Ed. James Bain. Hurtig, Edmonton, Alberta. B. Franklin, New York, 1969.

Hirbour, René. "Études de trois niveaux d'intégration sociale d'une société de chasseurs cueilleurs: Kitche-Zagik Anichenabe." Master's thesis, University of Montréal, Québec, 1969.

Hodge, Frederick W., ed. *Handbook of American Indians North of Mexico.* 2 vols. Bureau of North American Ethnology, Bulletin 30. Washington,

D.C., 1907–10. Reprint. New York: Bowman and Littlefield, 1971.

Jenness, Diamond. *The Indians of Canada.* Anthropological Series, no. 15, Bulletin 65. Ottawa, Ontario: National Museum of Man, 1967.

Johnson, Frederick. "An Algonquian Band at Lac Barrière, Province of Québec." Museum of the American Indian, Heye Foundation. *Indian Notes* 7, no. 1 (1930): 27–39.

———. "The Algonquin at Golden Lake, Ontario." Museum of the American Indian, Heye Foundation. *Indian Notes* 5, no. 2 (1928): 173–78.

Kanuck. "Bark Canoeing in Canada." *Lippincott's Magazine*, n. s., 4. 1882.

Kaye, Jonathan. "Lac Simon: Rapport Préliminaire." Paper presented at the Algonquian Conference, Montréal, Québec, 1976.

Kennedy, C. C. "Ancient Man: The Champlain Trail." In *Notes on the History of Renfrew County*, by Price and Kennedy. Pembroke, Ontario. 1961.

———. "Ancient Man in the Ottawa Valley." *The Pembroke Centennial Book.* Pembroke, Ontario. 1958.

———. "Archaic Hunters in the Ottawa Valley." *Ontario History* 54 (1962): 2.

———. "Charmstones of the Ottawa Valley." *Ontario History* 52 (1960): 1.

———. "The NRU Site." *Ontario History* 48 (1956): 4.

———. *Preliminary Report on the Morrison Island— 6 Site.* National Museums of Canada, Bulletin 205, 100–125. Ottawa, Ontario, 1966.

———. *The Upper Ottawa Valley.* Pembroke, Ontario: Renfrew County Council, 1970.

La Hontan, Louis Armand. *Nouveaux voyages de M. le baron de LaHontan, dans l'Amérique septentrionale.* La Haye, France: Chez les Frères l'Honore, 1703.

Lake, Ernest L. *Pioneer Reminiscences of the Upper Ottawa Valley Commemorating Triple Centennial Years of St. John the Evangelist Church, Eganville, Ontario.* Ottawa, Ontario: Le Droit, 1966.

Lemoine, Georges. *Dictionnaire français-algonquin.* Québec: L'Action Sociale, 1911.

———. *Le génie de la langue algonquine.* 15e Congrès International des Americanistes, vol. 2. 1906.

Lescarbot, M. *The History of New France.* 3 vols. Toronto, Ontario: The Champlain Society, 1907–14.

Long, John. *Voyages and Travels of an Indian Interpreter and Trader Describing the Manners and Customs of the North American Indians; with an Account of the Posts Situated on the River Saint Laurence, Lake Ontario, etc. and a Table Showing the Analogy Between the Algonkin and Chippeway Languages.* London, 1791.

Mackenzie, Alexander. *Voyages from Montréal, on the River St. Laurence, Through the Continent of North America, to the Frozen and Pacific Oceans in the Years 1789 and 1793; With a Preliminary Account of the Rise, Progress, and Present State of the Fur Trade of That Country.* London: T. Cadell, Jr., and W. Davies, 1801.

Marois, Roger J. M. *Les schèmes d'établissement à la fin de la préhistoire et au début de la période historique: le sud du Québec.* Collection Mercure, Dossier no. 17. Ottawa, Ontario: Commission archéologique du Canada, 1974.

Martineau, Donat. *Le Fort Témiscamingue.* Ville-Marie, Québec: Société d'Histoire du Témiscamingue, 1969.

Mason, Otis T., and Meriden S. Hill. "Pointed bark canoes of the Kutenai and Amur." *Report of the U.S. National Museum for 1899*, 532–37. Washington, D.C.: Smithsonian Institution, 1901.

Mathevet, Jean-Claude. *Ka Titc Jezos (Life of Christ).* Reprint. Amos, Québec: Les Missionnaires Oblats de Marie Immaculée, 1968.

———. "Mots Loups." Manuscript. Archives of Notre-Dame de Montréal, Montréal, Québec, 1750.

Maurault, Olivier. "Oka: Les vicissitudes d'une mission sauvage." *Revue Trimestrielle Canadienne* 16 (1930): 12–49.

McGee, J. T. "Family Hunting Grounds in the Kippewa Area, Québec." *Primitive Man* 24 (July 1951): 3.

McGregor, Ernest. *Algonquin Lexicon.* Maniwaki, Québec: River Désert Education Authority, 1987.

———. *Surrenders of Land on the Maniwaki Indian Reserve.* Maniwaki, Québec: River Désert Educational Authority.

McLean, John. *John McLean's Notes of a Twenty-five Years' Service in the Hudson Bay Territory (1849).* Edited by William Wallace. Toronto, Ontario: The Champlain Society, 1932.

Moore, Kermot A. *Kipawa: Portrait of a People.* Cobalt, Ontario: Highway Book Shop, 1982.

Nicholas, Louis. "Grammaire de la langue algonquine." Manuscript. Bibliothèque Nationale, Paris, 1672–74.

North Renfrew Times, Deep River, Ontario, June 20, 1956; December 11, 1963.

Ottawa Citizen, Ottawa, Ontario, July 29, 1958.

Parent, Armand. *The Life of Rev. Armand Parent, the First French-Canadian Ordained by the Methodist Church. Forty-seven Years' Experience in the Evangelical Work in Canada. Thirty-one Years in Connection with the Conference and Eight Years*

Among the Oka Indians. Toronto: William Briggs; Montréal: C. W. Coates, 1887.

Perrot, Nicholas. *Mémoire sur les moeurs, coustumes et relligion des sauvages de l'Amérique septentrionale (1717).* Leipzig and Paris: A. Franck, 1864.

Pembroke Observer, Pembroke, Ontario, December 11, 1963.

Petrullo, V. M. "Decorative Art on Birch Bark from the Algonquin of River du Lièvre Band." Museum of the American Indian, Heye Foundation. *Indian Notes* VI: 225–242, 1929.

Pilling, James Constantine. *Bibliography of the Algonkian Languages.* Bureau of American Ethnology, Bulletin 13. Washington, D.C., 1892.

Potherie, Bacqueville de la. *Histoire de l'Amérique septentrionale.* Paris, 1722.

River Désert Algonquin Band. *Tales from the River Désert.* Maniwaki, Québec: River Désert Band, 1976.

River Désert Education Authority. *Ondamitada Kakina Mamawe.* Maniwaki, Québec, 1982.

Roberts, Kenneth G., and Philip Shackleton. *The Canoe: A History of the Craft from Panama to the Arctic.* Toronto, Ontario: Macmillan of Canada, 1983.

Rogers, E. S., and Roger A. Bradley. "An Archaeological Reconnaissance in South-Central Québec, 1950." *American Antiquity* 19 (1953): 2.

Roy, Anastase. *Maniwaki et la Vallée de la Gatineau.* Ottawa, Ontario: Imprimeur du Droit, 1933.

Sagard-Théodat, Gabriel. *Histoire du Canada et voyages que les Frères Mineurs Recollects y ont faicts pour la conversion des infidèles depuis l'an 1615. Avec un dictionnaire de la langue huronne.* 4 vols. Paris: E. Tross, 1866.

Scott, W. *Report Relating to the Affairs of the Oka Indians.* Ottawa, Ontario: 1883.

Sowter, T. W. E. "Algonkin and Huron Occupation of the Ottawa Valley." *The Ottawa Naturalist* 23, no. 4 (July 1909): 61–68; 23, no. 5 (August 1909): 92–104.

Speck, Frank. "Boundaries and Hunting Groups of the River Désert Algonquin." Museum of the American Indian, Heye Foundation. *Indian Notes* 6, no. 2 (1929): 97–120.

———. "Divination by Scapulimancy Among the Algonquin of River Désert." Museum of the American Indian, Heye Foundation. *Indian Notes* 5, no. 2 (1928): 167–73.

———. "The Family Hunting Band as the Basis of Algonkian Social Organization." *American Anthropologist* 17, no. 2 (1914): 289–305.

———. "Family Hunting Territories and Social Life of Various Algonkian Bands of the Ottawa Valley." *Memoirs of the Canadian Geological Survey,* Anthropological Series 8, no. 70 (1915): 1–10.

———. "The Indians of Québec." *International Paper Monthly* (October 1927): 9–11.

———. Myths and Folk-Lore of the Timiskaming Algonquin and Timagami Ojibwa." *Memoirs of the Canadian Geological Survey,* Anthropological Series 9, no. 71 (1915): 1–27.

———. "River Désert Indians of Québec." Museum of the American Indian, Heye Foundation. *Indian Notes* 4, no. 3 (1927): 240–52.

Speck, Frank, and Loren C. Eiseley. "Significance of Hunting Territory Systems of the Algonkian in Social Theory." *American Anthropologist* 41, no. 2 (1939): 269–80.

Suite, Benjamin. "Canot d écorce." *Bulletin des recherches historiques* 22 (1916): 236–41.

———. *Trois-Rivières d'autrefois. Mélange historique: études éparses et inédites de Benjamin Sulte.* Montréal, Québec, 1918–34.

———. "The Valley of the Ottawa in 1613." *Ontario Historical Society, Papers and Records* 13 (1915): 31.

Taylor, Henry. *Grassroots Artisans.* Scarborough, Ontario: Consolidated Amethyst Communications, 1982.

Taylor, J. Garth. *Canoe Construction in a Cree Cultural Tradition.* Mercury Series, Paper 64. Ottawa, Ontario: National Museum of Man, 1980.

Thavenet, Abbé. "Dictionnaire Algonquin-Français." Manuscript. Oka, Québec, 1815(?).

Thwaites, R. G., ed. *The Jesuit Relations and Allied Documents: Travel and Explorations of the Jesuit Missionaries in New France, 1610–1791. . . .* 73 vols. Cleveland: The Burroughs Bros. Company, 1896–1901. Reprint. New York: Pageant, 1959.

Troyes, Chevalier de. "Voyage du Sieur de Troyes." Public Archives of Canada, Clairambault Collection, 1016 (1686): 409–52.

Vastokas, J., and R. K. Vastokas. *Sacred Art of the Algonkians.* Peterborough, Ontario: Mansard Press, 1973.

Voegelin, Charles F., and Erminie W. Voegelin. "Linguistic Considerations of Northeastern North America." In *Man in Northeastern North America,* edited by Frederick Johnson, 178–94. Papers of the Robert S. Peabody Foundation for Archeology 3, Andover, Massachusetts, 1946.

Waugh, F. W. "Canadian Aboriginal Canoes." *Canadian Field Naturalist* 33, no. 2 (May 1919): 23–33.

Wright, J. V. *Préhistoire du Québec.* Montréal, Québec: Editions Fides, 1980.

Index

David and Ernestine Gidmark offer a summer birchbark
canoe building course on the shore of Lake Superior.
For more information, please write to them at
Box 26, Maniwaki, Québec J9E 3B3